《环球时报》
双语阅读精选

陈 晴 编著

清华大学出版社
北京

本书所有文章均由环球时报提供。未经许可，不得以任何方式复制本书的任何部分。

本书封面贴有清华大学出版社防伪标签，无标签者不得销售。
版权所有，侵权必究。举报：010-62782989，beiqinquan@tup.tsinghua.edu.cn。

图书在版编目（CIP）数据

《环球时报》双语阅读精选 / 陈晴编著. —北京：清华大学出版社，2023.8 (2025.6重印)
　　ISBN 978-7-302-64010-3

　　Ⅰ.①环… Ⅱ.①陈… Ⅲ.①英语-汉语-对照读物②时事评论-中国-文集 Ⅳ.①H319.4：D

中国国家版本馆CIP数据核字（2023）第124874号

责任编辑：陈　健
封面设计：何凤霞
责任校对：赵琳爽
责任印制：曹婉颖

出版发行：清华大学出版社
　　　　网　　址：https://www.tup.com.cn，https://www.wqxuetang.com
　　　　地　　址：北京清华大学学研大厦A座　　邮　编：100084
　　　　社 总 机：010-83470000　　邮　购：010-62786544
　　　　投稿与读者服务：010-62776969，c-service@tup.tsinghua.edu.cn
　　　　质量反馈：010-62772015，zhiliang@tup.tsinghua.edu.cn
印 装 者：大厂回族自治县彩虹印刷有限公司
经　　销：全国新华书店
开　　本：148mm×210mm　　印　张：6.125　　字　数：175千字
版　　次：2023年8月第1版　　印　次：2025年6月第4次印刷
定　　价：38.00元

产品编号：101863-01

序 言

听说读写是学习语言,特别是学习外语的四项基本功。大量阅读是语言学习者熟悉用语习惯、改善思维方式、进一步学习写作的有效途径。英文报刊内容包罗万象,语言规范地道,是英语学习者提高英语阅读水平的良好素材。但是中国学生学习英语,不仅要能看懂外刊,还要能用英文介绍我们的实际生活和精神面貌,这就需要大量阅读国内权威的英文报纸。

《环球时报》(*Global Times*)是由人民日报社主办与出版的国际新闻报刊,创刊于1993年1月。2009年4月20日,《环球时报》英文版创刊。它是中国面向全国发行的英语综合性报纸,也是唯一向国外传达符合中国基本国情综合新闻的一份报媒,具有全球影响力。其语言质量也被全世界媒体普遍称赞。因此它是适合英语学习的权威阅读材料。

本书从科技、社会、文化、政经、外交等领域入手,选取了《环球时报》上的数十篇文章来打开读者的视野,提高读者的英语水平。这些文章题材多样,风格全面,有报道也有评论。读者不仅可以熟悉词汇、表达,获取信息,而且可以提高写作技巧,陶冶情操。

除原文外,本书的编者还精心为大家设置了背景简介、全文翻译、单词点津、难句解析和练习题共五个版块。读者不仅可以读懂文章的内容,还可以学习英语语法和词汇,深入了解相关的新闻知识点。练习题分为两部分,选择题重在考查读者对文章的理解是否准确,问答题则侧重进一步的研究和思考。本书还特别邀请英语母语者对每一篇文章的原文和单词点津进行朗读,为广大读者提供听力材料和朗读范本。

不仅很多国际考试,比如托福、雅思,会从英文报刊中选取文章,国内的英语考试,比如高考、大学英语四六级,也会从英文报刊中挑选出题内容。因此,阅读本书有助于学生养成良好的阅读习惯,提高英语水平和考试成绩。

最后,感谢吕蕾老师的大力支持。本书在编写过程中,北京美文苑文化发展有限公司参与了部分资料的整理,在此一并表示感谢。

目 录

第一部分 科技 Technology

第1篇 Research from China's LAMOST suggests Milky Way is older than believed
中国郭守敬望远镜观测结果表明银河系比人们认为的更古老 ... 1

第2篇 Fossil found on edge of the roof of the world reveals an owl active during the day 6 million years ago
"世界屋脊"发现的化石表明600万年前猫头鹰在白天活动 ... 6

第3篇 China's Zhurong rover finds evidence of water on Mars: researchers
研究人员：中国"祝融号"火星车发现火星上有水的证据 ... 10

第4篇 China's radio telescope detects first persistently active repeating fast radio burst from 3b light years away
"中国天眼"探测到首例30亿光年外持续活跃的重复快速射电暴 ... 14

第5篇 China marks a milestone in new-gen heavy-duty rocket devt with successful engine test
中国发动机测试成功，标志着新一代重型火箭研制的里程碑 ... 18

第6篇 Chinese institute to form virtual space collaborative editing platform based on metaverse
中国研究所将建成基于元宇宙的虚拟空间协同编辑平台 ... 21

第7篇 The best-preserved dinosaur embryo ever discovered has been found in China
中国发现了迄今为止保存最好的恐龙胚胎 ... 25

第8篇 Chinese major rocket maker envisions reusable Mars Express
中国主要火箭制造商设想可重复使用的火星快车 ... 29

第9篇 Chinese human genetic resources to be banned for use abroad: Ministry of Science and Technology
科技部：禁止向境外提供中国人类遗传资源 ... 32

III

第二部分 社会 / Society

第1篇 15 Asian elephants back in original habitat in Yunnan after 'exodus'
15头亚洲象"出走"后重返云南原栖息地 / 37

第2篇 Chinese scientists find new possible cause of dinosaur extinction by studying egg fossils
中国科学家对恐龙蛋化石的研究揭示恐龙灭绝新原因 / 41

第3篇 Rare large 'red mountain' discovered in Hoh Xil
可可西里发现罕见"红山脉" / 45

第4篇 Two gibbon species declared extinct in the wild in China due to excessive 'human activities'
由于过度的"人类活动",两种长臂猿在中国宣布灭绝 / 49

第5篇 Breathtaking rescue fixes satellite glitch and ensures 100% success rate of China's BDS deployment
惊心动魄修复卫星故障,确保中国北斗三号全球卫星导航系统部署100%成功 / 53

第6篇 Chinese scientists find high water content in lunar soil samples brought back by Chang'e-5 mission
中国科学家在嫦娥五号带回的月壤样品中发现高含量的水 / 57

第7篇 Beijing distributes emotion-sensing equipment to highway and cross-province bus drivers
北京为高速路、跨省运营驾驶员重点配发情绪感知设备 / 61

第8篇 China mulls increased penalties, employment ban on internet violators to better safeguard cybersecurity
中国考虑加大处罚力度,禁止网络违法者就业,更好保护网络安全 / 65

第9篇 Renowned professor witnesses remarkable progress in China's higher education that is deeply rooted in Chinese spirit and culture over last decade
深植于中国精神文化,知名教授见证中国高等教育十年来的显著发展 / 69

目录

| 第 10 篇 | Creativity, self-expression, flexible work culture drive Gen-Z's innovative approach to employment
创造力、自我表达、灵活的工作文化推动Z世代的创新就业方式 | 73 |

| 第 11 篇 | Revealing a confident, vigorous and real China via window of short videos on rural life
通过乡村生活短视频展示自信、活力和真实的中国 | 77 |

| 第 12 篇 | Behind a trending 'green horse' plushie produced by a Chinese museum was design team wanting to narrow distance between cultural relics and the younger generation
中国某博物馆推出的"绿马"玩偶走红的背后，蕴含着设计团队拉近文物与年轻一代距离的希望 | 81 |

| 第 13 篇 | More young people in China are seeking a career in rural areas and local communities, bringing with them knowledge, vitality
越来越多的中国青年怀揣知识与热情在乡村和社区街道就业 | 84 |

第三部分 文化 Culture

| 第 1 篇 | Chinese artists keep tradition alive with database of decorative patterns
中国艺术家建立装饰纹样数据库，让传统纹样重焕生机 | 89 |

| 第 2 篇 | Guizhou Province holds ethnic art festival to promote local intangible culture
贵州省举办民族艺术节，弘扬地方非物质文化 | 93 |

| 第 3 篇 | Ruins site spanning Neolithic age to Qing Dynasty discovered in East China
中国东部发现新石器时代至清代大型遗址 | 97 |

| 第 4 篇 | Never-before-seen bronze beast with four wings found at Sanxingdui Ruins
三星堆遗址发现首件四翼青铜兽 | 100 |

| 第 5 篇 | Chinese animation 100
中国动画100年 | 103 |

第6篇 China's village museum trend further advances rural revitalization
中国乡村博物馆更好赋能乡村振兴 / **106**

第7篇 New exhibition tackles climate action through art
新展览通过艺术参与气候行动 / **110**

第8篇 Chinese musicians seek to broaden traditional music's influence through creativity and international cooperation
中国音乐家们通过创意和国际合作扩大传统音乐的影响力 / **114**

第9篇 New exhibition in Beijing highlights Hong Kong urban design and development over past 25 years
北京新展呈现香港过去25年的城市设计和发展 / **117**

第10篇 Chinese vloggers promote traditional culture around the world by innovating on inheritance
视频博主通过传承创新在世界传播中国传统文化 / **120**

第11篇 'Qinqiang' inspired song cheers in e-sport game
"秦腔"主题曲唱响电子竞技游戏 / **124**

第四部分 政经 Politics and Economy

第1篇 China-built expressway in Nairobi, Kenya, starts trial operation
中国在肯尼亚内罗毕修建的快速路开始试运行 / **127**

第2篇 'Polar Silk Road' eyes new vision amid global challenges
"极地丝绸之路"在全球挑战中展现新愿景 / **131**

第3篇 China's national carbon market celebrates one year anniversary, becoming world's largest
中国全国碳市场一周年,成为全球最大碳市场 / **134**

第4篇 Dunhuang Research Institute, Tencent to launch digital scripture cave of Mogao Grottoes
敦煌研究院、腾讯将推出莫高窟数字藏经洞 / **137**

目录

第5篇 Space seed breeding makes breakthrough, yielding nearly 1,000 new species
太空育种取得突破，产生近 1,000 个新物种 / **141**

第6篇 Shanghai adopts China's 1st provincial-level AI law to support sound, safe development
上海通过中国人工智能领域的首部省级地方性法规，支持人工智能行业健康安全发展 / **145**

第7篇 China to cut soybean meal in livestock feed to ensure food security
中国将减少牲畜饲料中的豆粕，以确保粮食安全 / **148**

第8篇 Autonomous driving startups enhance tech innovation as industry gears up growth
随着行业加速发展，自动驾驶初创企业加强技术创新 / **152**

第9篇 NEVs penetration rate to reach 25% this year
今年，新能源汽车渗透率将达到 25% / **156**

第10篇 China's power supply, energy structure tested in extreme drought amid transition to cleaner energy future
在向清洁能源过渡期间，中国的电力供应、能源结构经受了极端干旱的考验 / **159**

第五部分 外交 Diplomacy

第1篇 Responsible neighbor: China maintains water release to downstream Mekong countries despite extreme heat, drought
负责任邻国：尽管遭遇旱情，中国仍继续向湄公河下游国家补水 / **163**

第2篇 China to play important role in further development of SCO: former Uzbek deputy prime minister
乌兹别克斯坦前副总理：中国将在上合组织进一步发展中发挥重要作用 / **167**

第3篇 China and Pakistan 'true brothers sharing weal and woe'
中巴是"患难与共的真兄弟" / **171**

| 第4篇 | Commemorative activities held to voice hope for a constructive China-Japan relation
各界举办纪念活动，对建设性中日关系表示期盼 | 174 |

| 第5篇 | LMC mechanism provides blueprint for successful bilateral relations as China, Myanmar treasure friendship: Myanmar politician
缅甸政治家：澜湄合作机制为中缅两国友好关系绘制了蓝图 | 178 |

| 第6篇 | Chinese UN representative reiterates opposition to bio weapons
中国常驻联合国代表重申：反对生物武器 | 182 |

参考答案 /185

Technology

第1篇

Research from China's LAMOST suggests Milky Way is older than believed

(2022.3.24)

Based on **monitoring** data collected by China's Large Sky Area **Multi-Object** Fiber Spectroscopic Telescope (LAMOST) and **European Space Agency** (ESA) Gaia Mission, **astronomers** have obtained the most accurate information so far concerning large samples of **stellar** ages, and their work suggests that the **Milky Way** is older than has long been believed.

They analyzed a survey of nearly 250,000 stars—**ranging** in age **from** 13.8 billion **to** 15 billion years—to track our galaxy's expansion by **cross-referencing** their lifecycles with the Milky Way's movements.

The **National Astronomical Observatories (NAOC)**, the Chinese Academy of Sciences, the operator of the LAMOST—a leading **optical** telescope project in China that is also known as the Guo Shoujing Telescope, **hailed** the development in a statement it provided to the *Global Times* on Thursday, saying the findings based on the large telescope in North China's Hebei Province clearly reconstructed images of the **formation** and **evolution** of the Milky Way during its "infancy and adolescence" in a **chronological** fashion.

一、背景简介

LAMOST，大天区面积多目标光纤光谱天文望远镜，又称郭守敬望远镜，是一架新类型的大视场兼备大口径望远镜，应用薄镜面主动光学加拼接镜面主动光学技术。它位于河北省兴隆县中国科学院国家天文台兴隆观测站。LAMOST 在大规模光学光谱观测和大视场天文学研究方面居于国际领先的地位。

为了理解银河系的形成，需要确定大量样本恒星的精确年龄。处于亚巨星演化阶段的恒星相当于一个精确的恒星钟，天文学家可根据其亮度，在短暂的恒星阶段精确测量其年龄。然而，由于这个演化阶段太短，对处于亚巨星阶段恒星的观测结果较少，之前也缺少大规模的测量数据。本文即讲述天文学家根据中国郭守敬望远镜和欧洲航天局盖亚空间天文台的数据，推测银河系准确年龄得出的新发现。研究结果表明，银河系可能经过了不同的演化阶段，其起点是约 130 亿年前盘族恒星的形成。

二、全文翻译

中国郭守敬望远镜观测结果表明银河系比人们认为的更古老

根据中国大天区面积多目标光纤光谱天文望远镜（LAMOST）和欧洲航天局（ESA）盖亚任务（Gaia Mission）收集的监测数据，天文学家获得了迄今为止最精确的大样本恒星年龄信息，他们的发现表明银河系比人们长期以来认为的更为古老。

天文学家对近 25 万颗恒星进行了分析，这些恒星的年龄从 138 亿年到 150 亿年不等，通过对恒星生命周期和银河系的运动进行交叉参考来追踪银河系的扩张。

中国科学院国家天文台（NAOC）、LAMOST（中国先进的光谱望远镜，又称郭守敬望远镜）运营商于周四在《环球时报》发表声明，对这一进展表示赞赏。声明中称，这项基于中国北部河北省大型望远镜的发现，以时间顺序清晰地再现了银河系在"幼年和青少年期"的形成和演化过程。

三、单词点津

1. **monitor** ['mɒnɪtə(r)] *v.* 监视、监听 *n.* 显示器，监控器

2. **multi-object** multi 作词缀表示"多个"的意思。object *n.* 目标、客体 *v.* 反对，比如想对对方观点表示不同意，就可以说"Object!"。

3. **ESA, European Space Agency** 欧洲航天局，是一个致力于探索太空的政府间组织，总部设在法国巴黎。

4. **astronomer** [ə'strɒnəmə(r)] *n.* 天文学家，词根是 astro-。同根词还有 astronomical *adj.* 天文的，astronomy *n.* 天文学，这个词还可以用来表达金额、数量等如天文数字般的，形容价格极其昂贵。

5. **stellar** ['stelə(r)] *adj.* 星球的。这个单词中，词根 -stell- 表示"星"，-ar 是形容词词尾。

6. **Milky Way** 银河，源于希腊神话。宙斯跟阿尔克墨涅生下了赫拉克勒斯。宙斯希望赫拉克勒斯将来能长生不老，就偷偷地把赫拉克勒斯放在女神赫拉身旁，想让他吃了赫拉的乳汁，变成长生不老之身。谁知赫拉克勒斯吮吸太猛，惊醒了赫拉。后者发现吃奶的不是自己的儿子，便一把将孩子推开，乳汁划过天际，便成了 Milk Way，银河。

7. **range from…to…** 表示范围从……到……

8. **cross-reference** *v.* 相互参照；交叉引用

9. **National Astronomical Observatories (NAOC)** 中国科学院国家天文台，成立于2001年4月，是由中国科学院北京天文台、云南天文台、南京天文光学技术研究所、乌鲁木齐天文站和长春人造卫星观测站等两台一所两站整合而成。

10. **optical** ['ɒptɪkl] *adj.* 光学的；视觉的

11. **hail** [heɪl] *v.* 赞扬，欢呼 *n.* 冰雹

12. **formation** [fɔː'meɪʃn] *n.* 构成，形成。其词根是动词 form。

13. **evolution** [ˌiːvə'luːʃn] *n.* 进化，演变，发展

14. **chronological** [ˌkrɒnə'lɒdʒɪkl] *adj.* 按发生时间顺序排列的，按时间计算的。同根词 chronicle *n.* 编年史。

四、难句解析

难句 1

Based on monitoring data **collected by** China's Large Sky Area Multi-Object Fiber Spectroscopic Telescope (LAMOST) and European Space Agency (ESA) Gaia Mission, astronomers have obtained the most accurate information so far concerning large samples of stellar ages.

 based on，定语前置，整个前半句都是后半句中 information 的修饰成分。

 collected 修饰前面的 data，因为 data 是被收集，所以用 ed 形式。

③ **have obtained**，现在完成时，表示过去的行为对现在有影响。

④ **concerning** 修饰前面的 information，information 和这个动词为主动关系，所以用 ing 形式。

难句 2

…the operator of the LAMOST—a leading optical telescope project in China that is also known as the Guo Shoujing Telescope,…

这个句子使用了同位语，破折号后面即是对 LAMOST 的补充说明，that 引导定语从句。

五、练习题

选择题

 _____ suggests that the Milky Way is older than has long been believed.

A. The data only collected through LAMOST

B. The large samples of stellar ages

C. The work of European Space Agency

D. The most accurate information so far

2. To be able to track our galaxy's expansion, we need to _____ nearly 250,000 stars, lifecycles with the Milky Way's movements.

   A. cross-reference

   B. cross-check

   C. cross-index

   D. illustrate

3. The Guo Shoujing Telescope clearly reconstructed images of the formation and evolution of the Milky Way during its "infancy and adolescence" in a chronological fashion. What would be the best vocabulary to replace "formation"?

   A. Development.

   B. Involvement.

   C. Establishment.

   D. Construction.

Do your research and answer these questions orally or by writing.

1. How important do you think the space research is to our country and why?

2. Do you believe in the near future humans will inhabit other planets and why?

Fossil found on edge of the roof of the world reveals an owl active during the day 6 million years ago

(2022.3.29)

A species of **diurnal** owls was identified from a piece of **fossil** found on northeastern edge of the Qinghai-Xizang **Plateau** in China, giving clues on how the diurnal birds evolved in the mostly **nocturnal** species.

Most owls living today are nocturnal, giving them a special status in myths of different cultures and **symbolize** magic due to the **popularity** of *Harry Potter* series.

A research team from the Institute of **Vertebrate Paleontology and Paleoanthropology** of the Chinese Academy of Sciences discovered the fossil in good state of **preservation**. The **specimen** is close to the northern hawk owl, a medium-sized owl of the northern **latitudes**, non-migratory and diurnal. The **extinct** owl belongs to clade Surniini which contains most living diurnal owl species.

A **comparison** of **sclera** bones of the **Miocene** owl and 55 reptiles and 360 birds, including many owls, showed the ancient bird's eyes are less open to light and enable it to see things clear during the day, according to a statement by the institute.

一、背景简介

猫头鹰是一种大家很熟悉的鸟类，在全球大部分地区都有分布，种类多达 130 多种，属于"鸮形目"。人们通常认为它们是夜行性的肉食性鸟类，白天躲起来睡觉，夜幕降临时才会开始活动。

本文讲述了研究人员在青藏高原发现了古老的猫头鹰化石，显示 600 万年前在这里曾经生活着一种有可能是世界上最古老的猫头鹰，在白天行动。这是通过对它们的"巩膜骨"研究得知的。"巩膜"是眼球壁的重要组成部分，也是可以帮助生物看清楚东西的关键部位之一。古猫头鹰的眼睛是可以削弱阳光的，而为什么经历了长期的进化，现代猫头鹰昼伏夜出，还需要更多的化石证据。

二、全文翻译

"世界屋脊"发现的化石表明600万年前猫头鹰在白天活动

在中国青藏高原东北缘发现的一块化石中，发现了一种昼行性的猫头鹰，这为研究昼行性鸟类如何进化为夜行性物种提供了线索。

当今大多数猫头鹰都是夜行性的，这使得它们在不同文化的神话中都有着特殊的地位，而且由于《哈利·波特》系列广为流行，猫头鹰甚至象征着魔法。

中国科学院古脊椎动物与古人类研究所的一个研究团队发现了这块保存完好的化石。该标本接近北鹰鸮——一种中等大小的北纬度猫头鹰，具有非迁徙性，并于昼间行动。这种已灭绝的猫头鹰属于猛鸮类，其中包含大多数现存的昼行性的猫头鹰物种。

研究报告中称，研究团队将此块中新世猫头鹰化石的巩膜骨与55种爬行动物及360多种鸟类（包括许多猫头鹰）的巩膜骨进行了比较。结果表明，这种古老鸟类的眼睛对光线的开放度较小，使其能够在白天看清东西。

三、单词点津

1. **diurnal** [daɪˈɜːnl] *adj.* 白天的；每日的 *n.* 日报，日刊
2. **fossil** [ˈfɒsl] *n.* 化石；僵化的事物 *adj.* 化石的；不变的，古老的
3. **plateau** [ˈplætəʊ] *n.* 高原；稳定期，停滞期 *v.* 趋于平稳，进入停滞期
4. **nocturnal** [nɒkˈtɜːnl] *adj.* （动物）夜间活动的；夜间发生的
5. **symbolize** [ˈsɪmbəlaɪz] *v.* 象征，用符号代表；采用象征，使用符号
6. **popularity** [ˌpɒpjuˈlærəti] *n.* 流行，普及，受欢迎。enjoy great popularity，享有盛誉
7. **vertebrate** [ˈvɜːtɪbrət] *n.* 脊椎动物 *adj.* 脊椎动物（有关）的；有脊椎的
8. **paleontology** [ˌpælɪɒnˈtɒlədʒɪ] *n.* 古生物学

⑨ **paleoanthropology** [ˌpeɪlɪəʊˈænθrəˈpɒlədʒɪ] *n.* 古人类学

⑩ **preservation** [ˌprezəˈveɪʃn] *n.* 保护，维护；保留

⑪ **specimen** [ˈspesɪmən] *n.* 样品，标本，抽样

⑫ **latitude** [ˈlætɪtjuːd] *n.* 纬度；回旋余地

⑬ **extinct** [ɪkˈstɪŋkt] *adj.* 灭绝的，消亡的

⑭ **comparison** [kəmˈpærɪsn] *n.* 比较，相提并论；比喻

⑮ **sclera** [ˈsklɪərə] *n.* [解剖] 巩膜

⑯ **Miocene** [ˈmaɪəsiːn] *adj.* 第三纪中新世的　*n.* 第三纪中新世。第三纪（Tertiary Period）是新生代的最老的一个纪（距今6,500万年~260万年）。中新世（英语：Miocene，符号：MI）为地质年代新近纪的第一个时期，开始于2,300万年前到533万年前。

四、难句解析

A species of diurnal owls was identified from a piece of fossil found on northeastern edge of the Qinghai-Xizang Plateau in China, giving clues on how the diurnal birds evolved in the mostly nocturnal species.

① **found** 是定语，修饰前面的 fossil。

② **giving clues on…**，在一个句子中，如果已经存在一个谓语动词，而又没有连词，其他的动词就需要使用非谓语形式。ing 形式表示主动、进行。

③ **mostly** 是副词，修饰 nocturnal。

The specimen is close to the northern hawk owl, a medium-sized owl of the northern latitudes, non-migratory and diurnal. The extinct owl belongs to clade Surniini which contains most living diurnal owl species.

① 第一句中，a medium-sized owl… 为 the northern hawk owl 的同位语，另外形容词（non-migratory and diurnal）后置，使句式生动，也突出了这个物种的特征。

② 第二句中 which 引导定语从句。

五、练习题

1. _____ indicates how the diurnal birds evolved in the mostly nocturnal species.

   A. The Qinghai-Xizang Plateau

   B. The northeastern edge of the Qinghai-Xizang Plateau

   C. A diurnal owl's fossil

   D. Owls that are alive today

2. Which of the following reasons is incorrect as to why owls symbolize magic and have a special status in myths?

   A. Because owls appear in the *Harry Potter* series.

   B. Because the *Harry Potter* series is popular.

   C. Because owls are in myths of different cultures.

   D. Because owls are active during daytime.

3. How can we tell the fossil found from the Qinghai-Xizang Plateau is diurnal and not nocturnal?

   A. Because they are from the northeastern edge of the Qinghai-Xizang Plateau.

   B. Because they found the fossil.

   C. Because they are diurnal.

   D. Because the ancient bird's eyes are less open to light and enable it to see things clear during the day.

Do your research and answer these questions orally or by writing.

1. What kind of information can we get from fossils?

2. Why do you think owls are used to deliver letters in *Harry Potter*?

China's Zhurong rover finds evidence of water on Mars: researchers

(2022.5.12)

Chinese researchers have **detected** water-bearing **minerals** on Mars by analyzing data collected by the country's Zhurong rover that is currently **trekking** on the surface of the Red Planet.

The research team with the Chinese Academy of Sciences' State Key Laboratory of Space Weather and the academy's Center for Excellence in Comparative Planetology led by fellow researcher Liu Yang, made analysis over Zhurong rover's data on **sediments** and minerals of the craft's site and concluded that evidence was found to suggest water persists on Mars.

Their findings have been published in details in the journal *Science* on Wednesday. And it marked a first around the world that water-bearing minerals on Mars have been detected by the shortwave **infrared spectrometer** on a Mars rover.

As part of China's Tianwen-1 Mars probe mission, Zhurong rover landed in a large plain in Mars' northern hemisphere called Utopia **Planitia** on May 15, 2021.

So far, Zhurong have been roving the landing site for a year and trekked nearly 2,000 meters on the Mars **surface**.

一、背景简介

祝融号是天问一号任务火星车。2020 年 7 月 23 日在中国文昌航天发射场由长征五号遥四运载火箭发射升空。2021 年 4 月 24 日，2021 年中国航天日开幕启动仪式在江苏南京举行，中国首辆火星车命名为"祝融号"，意为火神祝融登陆火星。其英文名称采用直接音译方式确定为"Zhurong"。2021年8月23日，祝融号火星车在火星平安度过第100天，更是行驶里程突破1,000米的关键一天。

中国科学院国家空间科学中心空间天气学国家重点实验室刘洋研究员团队利用祝融号火星车获取的短波红外光谱和导航与地形相机数据，在着陆区发现了岩化的板状硬壳层，通过分析光谱数据发现，这些类似沉积岩的板状硬壳层富含水硫酸盐等矿物。这标志着祝融号在国际上首次实现了利用巡视器上的短波红外光谱仪在火星原位探测到含水矿物的目标。这一发现对理解火星的气候环境演化历史具有重要意义。

二、全文翻译

研究人员：中国"祝融号"火星车发现火星上有水的证据

中国研究人员通过分析祝融号火星车收集的数据，探测到火星上的含水矿物。祝融号目前正在火星表面行走。

由研究员刘洋领导的中科院空间天气学国家重点实验室和中科院比较行星学卓越创新中心的研究团队，对祝融号着陆区沉积物和矿物的数据进行了分析，并得出结论：有证据表明火星上有水存在。

他们的详细研究结果已于周三在《科学》杂志上发表。这标志着世界上首次利用火星探测车上的短波红外光谱仪探测到火星上的含水矿物。

作为中国"天问一号"火星探测任务的一部分，2021年5月15日，祝融号火星车着陆在火星北半球一个名为"乌托邦平原"的大平原上。

截至目前，祝融号已经在着陆点漫游了一年，在火星表面跋涉了近2,000米。

三、单词点津

1. **detect** [dɪ'tekt] *v.* 查明，察觉；测出

2. **mineral** ['mɪnərəl] *n.* 矿物质 *adj.* （与）矿物（有关）的

3. **trek** [trek] *v.* （尤指徒步）长途跋涉；（尤指在山中）远足，徒步旅行 *n.* 一段路程；长途艰苦旅行

4 **sediments** ['sedɪmənts] *n.* 沉淀物 *v.* （液体）沉淀；沉积

5 **infrared** [ˌɪnfrə'red] *adj.* 红外线的 *n.* 红外区，红外线

6 **spectrometer** [spek'trɒmɪtə(r)] *n.* [光] 分光仪

7 **planitia** [plə'nɪʃə] *n.* 平原

8 **surface** ['sɜːfɪs] *n.* 表面；水面；台面 *v.* 浮出水面；（信息、情感或问题）显露，暴露 *adj.* 表面的；外表上的

四、难句解析

Chinese researchers have detected water-bearing minerals on Mars by analyzing data collected by the country's Zhurong rover that is currently trekking on the surface of the Red Planet.

1 句子中有 5 个介词。

2 **on the surface of sth.**，在……的表面。

3 第一个 by 表示"通过……手段/方法做某事"。

4 第二个 by 表被动，the data was collected by the rover。

五、练习题

1 Where did the Chinese researchers specifically find water on Mars?

   A. The collected data.

   B. The country's Zhurong rover.

   C. Minerals on Mars.

   D. The surface of the Red Planet.

[2] The word "trek" appears twice in the article, which of the following is the most similar meaning?

   A. Do research.

   B. Stay.

   C. Travel around.

   D. Excurse.

[3] What machine eventually found water-bearing minerals on Mars?

   A. China's Tianwen-1 Mars probe mission.

   B. The short-wave infrared spectrometer.

   C. The Chinese Academy of Sciences' State Key Laboratory of Space Weather.

   D. Zhurong rover.

Do your research and answer these questions orally or by writing.

[1] If you could move to Mars, what would you like to bring from home and why?

[2] Have you read any other books or articles about Mars? What have you learned?

China's radio telescope detects first persistently active repeating fast radio burst from 3b light years away

(2022.6.8)

An international team led by Chinese scientists discovered and located the first **persistently** active repeating fast radio burst (FRB) with the help of the world's largest radio telescope, China's Five-hundred-meter Aperture Spherical Radio Telescope (FAST), which **indicated** the evolution of FRBs and may help scientists understand the origin of the brightest radio waves **emanating** from billions of light years outside the **galaxy**.

The new FRB, named FRB190520B, was discovered in a metal-poor **dwarf** galaxy 3 billion light years away.

FRBs are **mysterious** radio flashes lasting **milliseconds** from deep space, but little is known about their origin although some scientists suggest that they could be evidence of advanced alien life.

So far, less than 5 percent of all the hundreds of FRBs detected have been seen to repeat. Only a few are active and only the newly discovered FRB190520B is persistently active, thus providing precious **glances** into their secrets.

一、背景简介

500米口径球面射电望远镜（Five-hundred-meter Aperture Spherical radio Telescope，FAST），又名"中国天眼"，位于中国贵州省黔南布依族苗族自治州境内，是中国国家"十一五"重大科技基础设施建设项目。该项目于2020年1月11日通过国家验收工作，正式开放运行。该望远镜开创了建造巨型望远镜的新模式，建设了反射面相当于30个足球场的射电望远镜，灵敏度达到世界第二大望远镜的2.5倍以上，大幅拓宽人类的视野，用于探索宇宙起源和演化。

本文讨论的快速射电暴（Fast Radio Bursts，FRB），是一种神秘的来自银河系外的射电天文现象。爆发的持续时间仅为几个毫秒，却可在这极短的时间内显示出极高的亮度，相当于太阳在一整天内释放的能量。快速射电暴的偏振性质包含快速射电暴本征特性与形成环境的丰富信息，对快速射电暴偏振性质的精确测量将继续推进对快速射电暴环境及其起源的理解进程。

二、全文翻译

"中国天眼"探测到首例30亿光年外持续活跃的重复快速射电暴

由中国科学家领导的国际团队利用世界上最大的射电望远镜——中国500米口径球面射电望远镜（FAST），发现并定位了首例持续活跃的重复快速射电暴（FRB），这表明了FRB的演化，有助于科学家了解从星系外数十亿光年发出的最亮无线电波的起源。

新的快速射电暴被命名为FRB190520B，定位于30亿光年外的一个贫金属矮星系。

快速射电暴是来自宇宙深处神秘的持续数毫秒的无线电闪光，尽管一些科学家认为它们可能是高级外星生命存在的证据，但对其起源知之甚少。

到目前为止，在检测到的数百个快速射电暴中，重复出现的不到5%。在只有少数快速射电暴是活跃的情况下，只有新发现的FRB190520B是持续活跃的，因此我们才能有宝贵契机窥见它们的秘密。

三、单词点津

1. **persistently** [pəˈsɪstəntlɪ] *adv.* 坚持地；固执地
2. **indicate** [ˈɪndɪkeɪt] *v.* 表明，象征，暗示。indicate left 打左转向灯
3. **emanate** [ˈeməneɪt] *v.* 产生；散发；表现出

4 **galaxy** ['ɡæləksi] *n.* 星系；银河，银河系

5 **dwarf** [dwɔːf] *n.* 小矮人，侏儒　*v.* 使显得矮小，使相形见绌　*adj.* 矮小的，矮种的

6 **mysterious** [mɪ'stɪəriəs] *adj.* 神秘的，不可思议的

7 **millisecond** ['mɪlisekənd] *n.* [计量]毫秒。milli 通常为"毫"单位的前缀。

8 **glance** [ɡlɑːns] *v.* 一瞥；浏览；击中……后弹开；反光　*n.* 一瞥；闪烁，闪耀

四、难句解析

FRBs are mysterious radio flashes lasting milliseconds from deep space, little is known about their origin although some scientists suggest that they could be evidence of advanced alien life.

1 **lasting milliseconds from deep space**，现在分词作定语。

2 **little is known about…** 表被动，主动形式为 people know little about…。

五、练习题

1 What is given this name FRB190520B?

   A. The first persistently active repeating fast radio burst.

   B. A metal-poor dwarf galaxy.

   C. All the hundreds of FRBs.

   D. Mysterious radio flashes lasting milliseconds from deep space.

2 Why can only the FRB190520B provide precious glances into FRBs' secrets?

   A. Because it could be evidence of advanced alien life.

B. Because the international team is led by Chinese scientists.

C. Because this one is detected by China's radio telescope.

D. Because only this one is consistently active.

3 According to the article, why are FRBs mysterious?

A. Because less than 5 percent of all the hundreds of FRBs detected have been seen to repeat.

B. Because they couldn't provide evidence of advanced alien life.

C. Because little is known about their origin.

D. Because they last milliseconds from earth.

Do your research and answer these questions orally or by writing.

1 Do you know how long a light year is? Do you have any idea how long billions of light years would be?

2 In order to become a space scientist, which subjects should we learn and what knowledge do we need to understand?

China marks a milestone in new-gen heavy-duty rocket devt with successful engine test

(2022.9.6)

China has successfully **conducted** a whole-craft running test for its 25 ton-level closed **expander** cycle **hydrogen-oxygen** rocket engine for the first time recently, which its developers claimed marked the world's largest scale testing for the kind and a key technology **breakthrough** for the country's development of the new-generation super heavy-lift launch **vehicle**.

The CASC revealed on its official website in December 2021 that the closed expander cycle hydrogen-oxygen rocket engine system has the advantages of high performance and high **reliability**, and has the ability of multiple starts and of large-scale **variable thrust** adjustment.

It can be used for complex space missions such as **manned** moon landing, manned Mars landing and deep space exploration, according to the CASC.

一、背景简介

中国航天科技集团六院 25 吨级闭式膨胀循环氢氧发动机首次整机热试车于 2022 年 9 月 5 日圆满成功，这是世界上最大规模的闭式膨胀循环发动机试车，标志着重型运载火箭关键技术之一的闭式膨胀循环氢氧发动机研制取得重大突破。

中国航天科技集团有限公司（简称"航天科技"或"中国航天"，英文名称：China Aerospace Science and Technology Corporation，缩写 CASC），是在中国战略高技术领域拥有自主知识产权和著名品牌、创新能力突出、核心竞争力强的国有特大型高科技企业。

二、全文翻译

中国发动机测试成功，标志着新一代重型火箭研制的里程碑

最近，中国首次成功地对其25吨级闭式膨胀循环氢氧发动机进行了整机运行试验，中国航天科技集团表示，这是世界上最大规模的此类测试，标志着中国研制新一代超重型运载火箭取得关键技术突破。

中国航天于2021年12月在其官网上透露，闭式膨胀循环氢氧发动机系统具有高性能和高可靠性的优点，具备多次启动和大范围可变推力调节能力。

中国航天表示，它可以用于复杂的太空任务，如载人登月、载人登火和深空探测等。

三、单词点津

1. **conduct** [kənˈdʌkt] *v.* 实施；带领 *n.* 行为，举止
2. **expander** [ɪksˈpændə] *n.* [电子][声]扩展器；膨胀器
3. **hydrogen-oxygen** 氢-氧
4. **breakthrough** [ˈbreɪkθruː] *n.* 突破，重大进展
5. **vehicle** [ˈviːəkl] *n.* 交通工具，车辆
6. **reliability** [rɪˌlaɪəˈbɪlɪti] *n.* 可靠性，可信度
7. **variable** [ˈveəriəbl] *adj.* 易变的，可变的，可调节的 *n.* 可变性；变量
8. **thrust** [θrʌst] *n.* 要点；刺；驱动力，推力 *v.* 猛推，猛塞
9. **manned** [mænd] *adj.* 载人的；有人驾驶的

四、练习题

1. What good qualities does the closed expander cycle hydrogen-oxygen rocket engine system have?

    A. Less labour and easy control.

B. Manpower and less cost.

C. Ease of repair and less power consumption.

D. Improved performance and high dependability.

2. Which of the following statements is correct?

A. China accomplished a whole-craft running test for its 25 ton-level closed expander cycle hydrogen-oxygen rocket engine.

B. China nearly completed a whole-craft running test for its 25 ton-level closed expander cycle hydrogen-oxygen rocket engine.

C. China successfully completed a whole-craft running test for its 25 ton-level open expander cycle hydrogen-oxygen rocket engine.

D. China failed to complete a whole-craft running test for its 25 ton-level closed expander cycle hydrogen-oxygen rocket engine.

3. Which word can replace "large-scale" in the article?

A. Small-scale.

B. Intensive.

C. Extensive.

D. Inclusive.

Do your research and answer these questions orally or by writing.

1. Why do we need to explore outer space so much?

2. In terms of the complex space missions, compared with human beings, what are the advantages and disadvantages of machines?

Chinese institute to form virtual space collaborative editing platform based on metaverse

(2021.12.16)

The Beijing Institute of Electronic Engineering will form a **virtual space collaborative** editing platform for **combat** mission design, based on new virtual environment **interaction** concepts such as metaverse and virtual twin, in order to provide a technical basis for multi-player collaborative scene editing for military training and other applications, according to a military requirement **announcement** released by the institution.

According to the announcement, the institution will carry out research on virtual twin and metaverse collaborative modeling and **simulation**, in order to explore ways to digitally connect equipment to metaverse **scenarios**.

Alongside the engineering institution, a number of Chinese internet giants have **scrambled** to join the metaverse, which is widely defined as an alternative digital reality where people work, play and socialize. The country's three online **behemoths** or "BAT" for Baidu, Alibaba and Tencent have got a head start, including registering related **trademarks** like "Ali Metaverse."

一、背景简介

元宇宙（Metaverse）是由 Meta 和 Verse 两个单词组成，Meta 表示超越，Verse 代表宇宙（universe），合起来即为"超越宇宙"的概念：一个平行于现实世界运行的人造空间，是互联网发展的下一个阶段，由 AR、VR、3D 等技术支持的虚拟现实的网络世界。

元宇宙一词诞生于 1992 年出版的科幻小说《雪崩》，小说描绘了一个庞大的虚拟现实世界,在这里,人们拥有自己的虚拟替身,相互竞争以提高自己的地位。元宇宙整合多种新技术,成为新型虚实融合的互联网应用和社会形态,基于扩展现实技术提供沉浸式体验,将虚拟世界与现实世界在经济系统、社交系统、身份系统上密切融合,并且允许每个用户进行内容生产和编辑。

二、全文翻译

中国研究所将建成基于元宇宙的虚拟空间协同编辑平台

根据北京电子工程总体研究所发布的军工需求公告,研究所将基于元宇宙、虚拟孪生等新型虚拟环境交互理念,构建为作战任务设计的虚拟空间协同编辑平台,为军事训练和其他应用中的多人协同场景编辑提供技术基础。

根据公告,该所将开展虚拟孪生和元宇宙协同建模与仿真研究,以探索将装备数字化接入元宇宙场景的方法。

除了该研究所,许多中国互联网巨头都争相进军元宇宙,元宇宙被广泛定义为人们工作、娱乐和社交的替代数字现实。中国互联网三大巨头,即百度、阿里巴巴和腾讯已经抢占先机,包括注册"阿里元宇宙"等相关商标。

三、单词点津

1. **virtual** [ˈvɜːtʃuəl] *adj.*(在计算机或互联网上存在或出现的)虚拟的,模拟的

2. **collaborative** [kəˈlæbərətɪv] *adj.* 合作的,协作的。动词形式为 collaborate。

3. **combat** [ˈkɒmbæt] *n.* 战斗,搏斗 *v.* 与……做斗争;防止,减轻

4. **interaction** [ˌɪntərˈækʃən] *n.* 互动,交流;相互作用。动词形式是 interact。

5. **announcement** [əˈnaʊnsmənt] *n.* 公告,宣布

6. **simulation** [ˌsɪmjuˈleɪʃn] *n.* 模拟,仿真;仿造物

7. **scenario** [sɪˈnɑːriːəʊ] *n.* 设想；电影、戏剧等的情节梗概，场景
8. **scramble** [ˈskræmbl] *v.* 爬，攀登；不规则地生长；仓促完成；争夺，抢夺 *n.* 攀爬；争夺
9. **behemoth** [bɪˈhiːmɒθ] *n.* 巨头；庞然大物
10. **trademark** [ˈtreɪdmɑːk] *n.* 商标；标志

四、难句解析

Alongside the engineering institution, a number of Chinese internet giants have scrambled to join the metaverse, which is widely defined as an alternative digital reality where people work, play and socialize.

1. **alongside the engineering institution**，介宾短语作状语。
2. **which** 引导非限定性定语从句，起补充说明作用，缺少也不会影响全句的理解。
3. **where people work, play and socialize**，where 为关系副词，引导定语从句。

五、练习题

1. What is the overall purpose of the research on virtual twin and metaverse collaborative modeling and simulation?

   A. For military training and other applications.
   B. For a military requirement announcement.
   C. Using the metaverse scenarios in a way that allows the connection of equipment through digital means.
   D. For combat mission design.

2. A number of Chinese internet giants have scrambled to join the metaverse. How would you understand "scramble" in this sentence?

   A. They all join the metaverse in a hurried way.

   B. They all join the metaverse in a competitive way.

   C. They all join the metaverse in a collaborative way.

   D. They all join the metaverse in a casual way.

3. What does "BAT" stand for?

   A. Best, Alternative and Trust.

   B. Baidu, Alibaba and Tencent.

   C. Battle, All Good and Threaten.

   D. Before, After and Tomorrow.

Do your research and answer these questions orally or by writing.

1. "The metaverse is widely defined as an alternative digital reality where people work, play and socialize." How do you envision this picture?

2. Do you believe the metaverse will fulfill most of our needs in the future, which means we can have a satisfactory digital lifestyle?

The best-preserved dinosaur embryo ever discovered has been found in China

(2021.12.22)

A dinosaur **embryo** perfectly preserved inside a fossil egg, the most complete **specimen** ever recorded in scientific studies, was found in China according to research by an international team of scientists.

The dinosaur embryo was discovered in rock **strata** of **the Late Cretaceous** in a site in Ganzhou, in East China's Jiangxi Province, and is now in the Yingliang Stone Natural History Museum in East China's Fujian Province.

The museum **nicknamed** the specimen Yingliangbeibei. The dinosaur embryo was preserved in a fairly **primitive** state, **undisturbed** by **fossilization**, and shows a clear picture of what it would have been like when it lived. The total length of the embryo is 27 centimeters and curls inside a 17-centimeter-long fossil egg.

一、背景简介

2021年12月22日，一件保存在恐龙蛋化石中的完美胚胎亮相福建省科技馆。该恐龙胚胎化石有着7,200万至6,600万年历史，是迄今为止科学记录的最完整的恐龙胚胎化石之一，揭示了恐龙胚胎与现代鸟类的密切联系。这只出生前的小恐龙看起来就像一只蜷缩在蛋里的小鸟，这又一次证明了今天鸟类的许多特征最早是从它们的恐龙祖先中演化出来的。该化石是在江西省赣州市的晚白垩世地层中发现的，属于一只没有牙齿的兽脚类恐龙，目前藏于福建省英良石材自然历史博物馆。

根据标本短高且无牙的头骨，其被确定为窃蛋龙类。该标本的保存姿势在已知的恐龙胚胎中是独一无二的，其头部位于身体下方，脚在两侧，身体背部沿着蛋的钝端蜷缩着。这种姿势与现代鸟类的胚胎类似，而在以前的恐龙胚胎化石中从来没有发现过这种情况。极少数恐龙蛋内保存有胚胎化石，是最稀有的化石之一，这些化石为研究恐龙的生殖、行为、演化以及古生态提供了宝贵资料。

二、全文翻译

中国发现了迄今为止保存最好的恐龙胚胎

根据某国际科学家团队的研究，在中国发现了一个完好保存在化石蛋中的恐龙胚胎，这是科学研究记录到的最完整的标本。

恐龙胚胎是在中国东南部江西省赣州市一处遗址的晚白垩世岩层中发现的，现藏于中国东南部福建省英良石材自然历史博物馆。

博物馆为此标本取名"英良贝贝"。恐龙胚胎保存状态相当原始，未受化石化作用的干扰，且清晰展现了其存活时的状态。胚胎的总长度为27厘米，蜷缩在一个长17厘米的恐龙蛋化石内。

三、单词点津

1. **embryo** ['embriəʊ] *n.* 胚，胚胎 *adj.* 胚胎的；初期的。sth. in embryo 某事在筹备中

2. **strata** ['strɑ:tə] *n.* 层；[地质]地层；阶层。rock strata 岩层

3. **the Late Cretaceous** 晚白垩世。晚白垩世，指白垩纪时期，早白垩世后面的阶段。此时期前期，恐龙依然兴盛。然而在最后的一年（6,500万年前），小行星与地球相撞，发生猛烈大爆炸，大量尘埃抛入大气层中，致使数月之内阳光被遮挡，植物枯死，食物链中断，包括恐龙在内的很多动物绝灭。

4. **nickname** ['nɪkneɪm] *v.* 给……起绰号 *n.* 绰号，外号

5. **primitive** ['prɪmətɪv] *adj.* 原始的，远古的；（器物等）粗糙的；本能的 *n.* 未开化的土人；原始派艺术家（或其作品）

6. **undisturbed** [ˌʌndɪ'stɜ:bd] *adj.* 未受干扰的；不受……影响的

7. **fossilization** [ˌfɒsəlaɪ'zeɪʃn] *n.* 石化；僵化；考古中是"化石化

作用"的意思，指将古代生物遗体、遗迹保存成化石的各种作用，包括古代生物遗体、遗迹被沉积物掩埋、保存、石化以及模铸形成等各种作用。

四、难句解析

The dinosaur embryo was preserved in a fairly primitive state, undisturbed by fossilization, and shows a clear picture of what it would have been like when it lived.

1. **was preserved** 表示该句为被动句，后面的 undisturbed by fossilization，是对 primitive state 的补充说明。
2. **like** 此处是介词，意为"像……"。

五、练习题

1. According to this article, what is the record created in China?

   A. A dinosaur embryo.

   B. An international team of scientists.

   C. The most complete specimen of a dinosaur embryo.

   D. A fossil egg.

2. What period of time is the embryo estimated to be from?

   A. Cretaceous.

   B. Triassic.

   C. Infancy.

   D. Crustacean.

3. Which of the following statements is correct?

   A. The fossil embryo was found in rock.

   B. The fossil embryo was found in sand.

C. The fossil embryo was found in water.

D. The fossil embryo was found in mud.

Do your research and answer these questions orally or by writing.

1. Why should we keep endangered animals alive and ensure they do not go extinct?

2. If the dinosaurs lived today, do you think they would be a great threat to human beings? Why or why not?

Chinese major rocket maker envisions reusable Mars Express

(2022.2.17)

Postgraduates of China's largest developer and producer of **carrier rockets** the China Academy of Launch Vehicle Technology (CALT) have **envisioned** a **reusable** transport system that will commute between a future space station in the Mars **orbit** and the **outpost** facility on the surface of the Red Planet.

China's first-ever independent **interplanetary** mission Tianwen-1 reached Mars in February 2021. And as China's space industry marks the first anniversary of the mission, the CALT postgraduates are celebrating by coming up with such a **futuristic** idea.

The distance between Earth and Mars is some 65 million kilometers at closest and some 400 million kilometers at farthest. It took Tianwen-1 295 days to reach Mars from Earth. And if we want to build a base on Mars, it is **prerequisite** to have such transport to make large-scale Earth-Mars transport and the probe and exploitation of the Red Planet a reality, said Liu Wenjie, one of the CALT postgraduates involved in the project's designing work.

一、背景简介

天问一号是由中国航天科技集团公司下属中国空间技术研究院抓总研制的探测器，负责执行中国第一次自主火星探测任务。天问一号于 2020 年 7 月 23 日在文昌航天发射场由长征五号遥四运载火箭发射升空，于 2021 年 2 月到达火星附近，实施火星捕获。2021 年 5 月软着陆火星表面，开展巡视探测等工作，实现中国在深空探测领域的技术跨越。深空探测将推动空间科学、空间技术、空间应用全面发展，为服务国家发展大局和增进人类福祉做出更大贡献。2022 年 2 月 4 日，天问一号在轨运行 561 天，在火星祝贺北京冬奥会盛大开幕。

本文讲述了中国运载火箭技术研究院的学生，为纪念天问一号一周年，提出的在地球和火星之间运行摆渡车的设想。

二、全文翻译

中国主要火箭制造商设想可重复使用的火星快车

中国运载火箭技术研究院（CALT）（中国最大的运载火箭研发和生产单位）的研究生们设想了一种可重复使用的运输系统，该系统将在未来火星轨道上的空间站和火星表面的前哨基地之间往返。

2021 年 2 月，负责执行中国首次独立星际探测任务的"天问一号"探测器抵达火星。在中国航天领域纪念天问绕火一周年之际，中国运载火箭技术研究院的研究生们提出这一设想以表庆祝。

地球与火星之间的最近距离约 6,500 万公里，最远约 4 亿公里。天问一号用了 295 天从地球到达火星。参与该项目设计工作的研究生柳文杰表示，如果我们想在火星上建立基地，那么拥有这样的运输工具是实现大规模地火运输以及探测和开发火星的先决条件。

三、单词点津

1. **carrier rocket** 运载火箭，航天运载工具的一种，是将有效载荷按照预定的速度和方向送入太空的火箭。

2. **envision** [ɪnˈvɪʒn] *v.* 想象，预想

3. **reusable** [ˌriːˈjuːzəbl] *adj.* 可以再度使用的，可重复使用的

4. **orbit** [ˈɔːbɪt] *n.* （环绕地球、太阳等运行的）轨道；影响范围 *v.* 沿轨道运行

5. **outpost** [ˈaʊtpəʊst] *n.* 前哨；偏远村镇

6. **interplanetary** [ˌɪntəˈplænɪtri] *adj.* 行星间的。interplanetary travel 星际旅行

7. **futuristic** [ˌfjuːtʃəˈrɪstɪk] *adj.* 极其现代的；（思想、书、影片等）幻想未来的。future 的形容词形式，同根词还有 futurist *n.* 未来学家

8 **prerequisite** [ˌpriːˈrekwəzɪt] *n.* 先决条件；前提

四、练习题

1 According to the article, what is a futuristic idea in order to inhabit mars?

   A. A future space station in the Mars orbit.

   B. The exploitation of the Red Planet.

   C. The one-year anniversary.

   D. A reusable transport system.

2 What does the word "envision" mean in the article?

   A. Hope.

   B. Demand.

   C. Conceive.

   D. Indicate.

3 According to the article, if we want to build a base on Mars, it is _____ to have such transport to make large-scale Earth-Mars transport and the probe as well as exploitation of the red planet possible.

   A. important

   B. a precondition

   C. fantastic

   D. requirement

Do your research and answer these questions orally or by writing.

1 Why is interplanetary transportation important?

2 In your opinion, how quickly will the interplanetary transportation take to get from earth to some other planets?

Chinese human genetic resources to be banned for use abroad: Ministry of Science and Technology

(2022.3.23)

Chinese human **genetic** resources will be banned for use abroad, China's Ministry of Science and Technology **stipulated** in its draft rules for the implementation of the **regulations** on the management of human genetic resources. The **proposal** was released on Tuesday for public consultation.

Human genetic resources refer to the genetic materials, such as organs, tissues and cells, which contain **hereditary** substances such as human genome and genes, according to the rules for the implementation of the regulations.

The plan stipulates that the collection, storage, **utilization** and supply of Chinese human genetic resources outside China should respect the **privacy** rights of the providers of human genetic resources and obtain consent in advance to ensure their health and protect their **legitimate** rights.

The activities of collection, storage and supply of Chinese human genetic resources conducted within China for use abroad must be carried out by Chinese scientific research institutions, colleges, medical institutions and enterprises.

一、背景简介

人类遗传资源是可单独或联合用于识别人体特征的遗传材料或信息，是开展生命科学研究的重要物质和信息基础，是认知和掌握疾病的发生、发展和分布规律的基础资料，是推动疾病预防、干预和控制策略开发的重要保障，已成为公众健康和生命安全的战略性、公益性、基础性资源。

我国生物医药创新能力和全球化进程飞跃式提升，对人类遗传资源管理服务能力提出新挑战、新要求。党的十八大以来，我国生物医药创新研发快速发展，对人类遗传资源的需求越来越大，涉及人类遗传资源的采集、保藏、国际合作科学研究活动等呈爆发式激增，行政许可申报数量和咨询数量呈指数倍增加，但仍有少数单位和个人法治意识淡薄，违法开展涉及人类遗传资源活动的情况时有发生。推动人类遗传资源有效保护和合理利用，对于保障个人权益、维护社会公共利益和筑牢国家生物安全屏障具有重要意义。

二、全文翻译

科技部：禁止向境外提供中国人类遗传资源

科技部在《人类遗传资源管理条例实施细则（征求意见稿）》中规定，将禁止向境外提供我国人类遗传资源，该提案于周二发布，面向社会公开征求意见。

根据实施细则，人类遗传资源材料是指含有人体基因组、基因等遗传物质的器官、组织、细胞等遗传材料。

该细则规定，采集、保藏、利用、对外提供中国人类遗传资源，应尊重人类遗传资源提供者的隐私权，并事先征得知情同意，以确保提供者健康并保护其合法权利。

在中国境内采集、保藏和对外提供中国人类遗传资源，必须由中国科研机构、高等学校、医疗机构和企业开展。

三、单词点津

1. **genetic** [dʒəˈnetɪk] *adj.* 基因的；遗传学的。genic disease 基因病
2. **stipulate** [ˈstɪpjuleɪt] *v.* 规定，明确要求。名词形式是 stipulation。
3. **regulation** [ˌreɡjuˈleɪʃn] *n.* 规章制度，规则
4. **proposal** [prəˈpəʊzl] *n.* 提议；建议；求婚。动词形式是 propose。
5. **hereditary** [həˈredɪtri] *adj.* （特点或疾病）遗传的；（头衔、职位或权利）承袭的，世袭的

6　**utilization** [ˌjuːtəlaɪˈzeɪʃn] *n.* 利用，使用。

7　**privacy** [ˈprɪvəsi] *n.* 隐私；秘密。right of privacy 隐私权

8　**legitimate** [lɪˈdʒɪtɪmət] *adj.* 正当的；合法的，依法的

四、难句解析

Human genetic resources refer to the genetic materials, such as organs, tissues and cells, which contain hereditary substances such as human genome and genes, according to the rules for the implementation of the regulations.

1　**which** 引导非限定性定语从句，修饰前面的 organs, tissues and cells。

2　**according to…** 介词词组，在句子中作原因状语，可放在句首或句末。

五、练习题

1　What are included in Chinese human genetic resources?

　A. Chinese scientific research institutions, colleges, medical institutions and enterprises.

　B. The genetic materials, such as organs, tissues and cells.

　C. The activities of collection, storage and supply.

　D. The implementation of the regulations on the management of human genetic resources.

2　Which organization set up the rule of "the Chinese human genetic resources will be banned for use abroad"?

　A. Its draft rules for the implementation.

B. China's Ministry of Science and Technology.

C. The activities of collection.

D. Chinese scientific research institutions.

3 According to the article, why have Chinese genetic resources been banned for use abroad?

A. Chinese genetic resources may be improperly used.

B. The Chinese genetic resources are unique.

C. Transporting Chinese genetic resources is complicated.

D. In order to respect the privacy rights of the providers of human genetic resources.

Do your research and answer these questions orally or by writing.

1 In your opinion, how important is the research from the article and how can it be used to help sick people?

2 How can this type of research mentioned in the article help people in other ways besides illness?

扫一扫，听音频

第二部分 社会
Society

15 Asian elephants back in original habitat in Yunnan after 'exodus'

(2022.9.20)

The 15 wild Asian elephants that went on a 1,400-kilometer "**exodus**" in 2021 in Southwest China's Yunnan Province are now back in their original habitat in Xishuangbanna and the two **calves** born during their trek have grown to 300 kilograms, **the National Forestry and Grassland Administration** revealed on Monday.

The herd of Asian elephants came into the global **spotlight** in 2021 after their unusual **northward** journey since April 2021.

The elephants returned to their original habitat in Xishuangbanna after the 124-day **trek** which **covered a distance of** over 1,400 kilometers, said Li Chunliang, deputy director of the National Forestry and Grassland Administration, during a **press conference** on Monday.

At the Monday conference, Li presented a photo taken of four elephants including two calves which drew much public attention back in 2021 because they were born during the trek. The photo was taken by **frontline** monitoring staff.

一、背景简介

"陆地巨无霸"亚洲象为我国一级重点保护野生动物,主要分布在云南普洱、西双版纳、临沧3个州市,是亚洲现存最大和最具代表性的陆生脊椎动物,也是维持森林生态系统平衡的"工程师"。1988年,《中华人民共和国野生动物保护法》颁布后,野生动物得到了很好的保护,亚洲象种群数量稳定增长,从20世纪80年代末的180多头,发展到现在的300多头。2021年4月16日,原生活栖息在西双版纳国家级自然保护区的15头亚洲象群向北迁移,10月重回到西双版纳范围内,12月回到了保护区,此事引起了全球关注。

二、全文翻译

15头亚洲象"出走"后重返云南原栖息地

国家林业和草原局周一透露,2021年,15头野生亚洲象在中国西南部的云南省"出走"1,400公里,现在它们已经回到了西双版纳的原栖息地。在长途跋涉中出生的两只象宝宝已重达300公斤。

亚洲象群在2021年4月开始了它们不同寻常的北上之旅,成为当年全球关注的焦点。

国家林业和草原局副局长李春良在周一的新闻发布会上表示,经过长达124天、1400公里的长途跋涉,象群返回了它们原来的栖息地西双版纳保护区。

会上,李春良展示了四头亚洲象的一张照片,其中包括两头幼象。两头幼象是在象群长途跋涉中出生的,在2021年引发广泛关注。照片由前线监测人员拍摄。

三、单词点津

1. **original** [ə'rɪdʒɪnəl] *adj.* 原先的;独创的,新颖的　*n.* 原件;原稿
2. **habitat** ['hæbɪtæt] *n.* (动植物的)生活环境,栖息地
3. **exodus** ['eksədəs] *n.* 大批的离去。本词中,前缀 ex 表示"向外";词根 od 表示"路"。

④ **calf** [kɑːf] *n.*（象、鲸等的）崽，幼兽。复数形式为 calves。

⑤ **the National Forestry and Grassland Administration** 国家林业和草原局

⑥ **spotlight** [ˈspɒtlaɪt] *n.* 聚光灯，反光灯；媒体和公众的注意。come into spotlight 引起注意

⑦ **northward** [ˈnɔːθwəd] *adj.* 向北的　*adv.* 向北地

⑧ **cover a distance of** 后接长度，表示距离。

⑨ **press conference** 新闻发布会

⑩ **frontline** [ˈfrʌntlaɪn] *n.* 前线

四、难句解析

Li presented a photo taken of four elephants including two calves which drew much public attention back in 2021 because they were born during the trek.

① **taken** 过去分词表被动，主动形式为 take a photo of four elephants。

② **including two calves** 作状语，后面 which 引导限制性定语从句，只修饰 two calves。

五、练习题

① Among the four choices below, what is the best explanation of the "exodus" from this article?

A. The 15 wild Asian elephants are now back in their original habitat.

B. A group of animals go out to play together.

C. A journey by a large group to escape from a hostile environment.

D. 15 elephants are in the same group.

2. What are the "two calves" in the article?

   A. The babies of the wild elephants.

   B. 300 kilograms.

   C. Their original habitat.

   D. The elephants' partners.

3. According to the article, which of the following reasons is incorrect as to what caused the herd of Asian elephants to come into the global spotlight in 2021?

   A. Because the group of Asian elephants went on a 1,400-kilometer "exodus".

   B. Because their 124-day trek covered a distance of over 1,400 kilometers.

   C. Because of their unusual northward journey.

   D. Because the Asian elephants' two calves have grown to 300 kilograms.

Do your research and answer these questions orally or by writing.

1. There is a lot of media coverage about the elephant's journey. Have you read a lot of the media coverage and what do you think about their journey?

2. As a human being, what should we do along with the elephants' trek? Should we protect them, feed them, guide them, or escort them to a zoo? If anything else, what do you think we should do?

Chinese scientists find new possible cause of dinosaur extinction by studying egg fossils

(2022.9.20)

Chinese scientists have discovered that a **sustained** decline in dinosaur **diversity** happened in **the Late Cretaceous period** by carrying out studies on dinosaur egg fossils.

They concluded that such decline **weakened** the dinosaurs' ability to adapt to environmental **upheavals derived** from major natural disasters which eventually caused their extinction.

Scientists have never stopped seeking the reason for the **disappearance** of dinosaurs, one of the most fascinating **paleontological** species to the public. These animals appeared in **the Late Triassic Epoch**, 235 million years ago, and lived on earth for as long as 170 million years but disappeared 66 million years ago.

The most prominent of the various **hypotheses** about the extinction of the dinosaurs include **extraterrestrial** factors, such as one involving the **asteroid** impact, as well as terrestrial factors, such as the massive volcanic **eruptions** in **India's Deccan Traps**. All these hypotheses are related to major geological events.

一、背景简介

6,600万年前，雄霸地球的恐龙消失了。什么原因导致了恐龙的灭绝？是小行星撞地球，是气候变化，还是大面积火山爆发？答案或许没这么简单。恐龙蛋作为恐龙在地球上繁衍生息的主要载体，不仅可以反映恐龙的繁殖习性，其在地层中的富集埋藏规律也能反映恐龙生存时期的古环境信息。来自中国科学院古脊椎动物与古人类研究所、中国科学院地质与地球物理研究所和中国地质大学（武汉）等机构的科学家对陕西山阳盆地恐龙化石开展了系统性研究，提出了一种恐龙灭绝可能的新机制：在晚白垩世时期，随着自然生态系统和恐龙自身的协同演化，恐龙多样性发生了持续性衰退，降低了恐龙这个类群的环境适应能力，导致其无法在由火山爆发或小行星撞击等重大灾害事件所引起的环境剧变中生存和复苏，最终走向灭绝。

二、全文翻译

中国科学家对恐龙蛋化石的研究揭示恐龙灭绝新原因

中国科学家通过对恐龙蛋化石的研究发现恐龙多样性在晚白垩世时期持续性衰退。

研究人员得出结论，恐龙多样性衰退削弱了恐龙适应由重大自然灾害导致的环境剧变的能力，而这些自然灾害最终导致了恐龙的灭绝。

恐龙是人们最感兴趣的古生物物种之一，科学家从未停止过寻找恐龙消失的原因。恐龙出现于2.35亿年前的晚三叠纪，在地球上生活了1.7亿年，但在6,600万年前灭绝。

关于恐龙灭绝的各种假说中，最流行的包括地外因素，如小行星撞击，以及陆地因素，如印度德干地盾的大规模火山爆发。这些假设都与重大地质事件有关。

三、单词点津

1. **sustained** [səs'teɪnd] *adj.* 持续的，持久的；坚持不懈的。动词 sustain（维持）的过去式和过去分词。

2. **diversity** [daɪ'vɜːsəti] *n.* 多样性；差异。cultural diversity 文化多元性

3. **the Late Cretaceous period** 晚白垩纪时期

4. **weaken** ['wiːkən] *v.* （使）虚弱，（使）衰弱；动摇，犹豫。weaken the ability 削弱能力

⑤ **upheaval** [ʌpˈhiːvl] *n.* 激变，剧变；（地壳）隆起

⑥ **derive** [dɪˈraɪv] *v.* 获得，取得；起源于，来自。derive from 源自，来自

⑦ **disappearance** [ˌdɪsəˈpɪərəns] *n.* 消失，失踪；消亡，灭绝。动词形式是 disappear。

⑧ **paleontological** [ˌpælɪɒntəˈlɒdʒɪkl] *adj.* 古生物学的

⑨ **the Late Triassic Epoch** 晚三叠纪

⑩ **hypotheses** [haɪˈpɒθəsiːz] *n.* 假说，假设；臆测（hypothesis 的复数）

⑪ **extraterrestrial** [ˌekstrətəˈrestriəl] *adj.* 地球外的   *n.* 天外来客

⑫ **asteroid** [ˈæstərɔɪd] *n.* 小行星

⑬ **eruption** [ɪˈrʌpʃ(ə)n] *n.* 喷发；（战争、怒气等的）爆发。volcanic eruptions 火山喷发

⑭ **India's Deccan Traps** 印度德干地盾，地表上最大型的火山地形之一。

四、难句解析

Scientists have never stopped seeking the reason for the disappearance of dinosaurs, one of the most fascinating paleontological species to the public.

① **stop doing** 和 stop to do 是有区别的。stop doing sth. 是"停止做某事"，其中 doing 是 stop 的宾语，是要停止的动作；stop to do sth. 是"停下来开始做某事"，to do 是 stop 的状语，表示目的，是要开始做的事情。

② **one of the most** + *adj.* + 名词复数形式，表示"最……的……之一"。

五、练习题

1. What impairs the dinosaurs' ability to adapt to environmental upheavals?

   A. The discovery from Chinese scientists.

   B. The continuing decrease of dinosaur diversity.

   C. The Late Cretaceous period.

   D. The most prominent of the various hypotheses.

2. Which speculation is excluded from the various hypotheses about the extinction of the dinosaurs?

   A. Massive volcanic eruptions.

   B. An asteroid impact.

   C. Extraterrestrial factors.

   D. One of the most fascinating paleontological species.

3. What does "eventually" mean in the article?

   A. Finally.

   B. Eventful.

   C. By all means.

   D. Variety.

Do your research and answer these questions orally or by writing.

1. Besides information in the article, what else do you know about dinosaurs?

2. In your opinion, why have scientists never stopped seeking the reason for the disappearance of the dinosaurs?

第3篇

Rare large 'red mountain' discovered in Hoh Xil

(2022.7.19)

A Chinese **expedition** recently discovered a large "red mountain" in Hoh Xil, in Northwest China's Qinghai Province, which could be dated back to the late Cretaceous or **Paleogene** period between 70 and 30 million years ago.

"It is rare to find such large, exposed area of red **strata** in China," said Shen Tianyi, associate professor at the School of Earth Sciences of the China University of Geosciences in Wuhan and one of the members of the expedition, **hailing** it as a "spectacular ancient **geological** relic" on the Qinghai-Xizang Plateau.

Sitting in the middle of Hoh Xil, the **mahogany** colored mountain is very **noticeable** in the green grassland of the basin in summer, with clear and **overlapping stratum** visibly exposed.

The mountain located in an east-to-west axis has clear **stratigraphic** sections and **asymmetric** slopes, **steep** in the south and slow in the north. Some 160 kilometers from north to south and nearly 600 kilometers from east to west of the stratums are naturally exposed.

一、背景简介

地处青藏高原的可可西里是我国最大的无人区。地质研究发现，在距今 3,000 多万年前，可可西里海拔很低，处于大型湖泊状态。后随着青藏高原隆升，可可西里随之抬升形成山间盆地。红色岩石在可可西里盆地分布广泛，北至五道梁地区，南至唐古拉山镇南侧，向西可延伸到西金乌兰湖以西地区，向东可到通天河沿线。这一次我国科考队在可可西里发现一处当地罕见的大规模红山脉，其包含的丰富地质信息将为深入研究青藏高原的演化提供重要的支持。

二、全文翻译

可可西里发现罕见"红山脉"

中国科考队最近在中国西北部青海省可可西里发现了一座大规模"红山脉"，其形成时间可追溯至 7,000 万至 3,000 万年前的白垩纪晚期或古近纪。

中国地质大学（武汉）地球科学学院副教授、科考队员申添毅说："红色地层出露面积之大在国内罕见。"他称赞这是青藏高原上一处"壮观的古地质遗迹"。

位于可可西里中部的红褐色山体在夏季绿色的草原盆地上非常显眼，山体上地层清晰，呈现出层叠状态。

山脉呈近东西走向，地层剖面裸露清楚，两坡不对称，南陡北缓。红色地层南北自然露出宽度超过 160 公里，东西延伸长度近 600 公里。

三、单词点津

1. **expedition** [ˌekspəˈdɪʃn] *n.* 远征，考察；探险队，考察队
2. **Paleogene** [ˈpæliədʒiːn] *n.* （地质学）古近纪，早第三纪
3. **hail** [heɪl] *v.* 赞扬，欢呼；招呼；下冰雹 *n.* 冰雹
4. **geological** [ˌdʒiːəˈlɒdʒɪkl] *adj.* 地质的，地质学的
5. **mahogany** [məˈhɒɡəni] *n.* 红木；红褐色
6. **noticeable** [ˈnəʊtɪsəbl] *adj.* 显而易见的，明显的；值得注意的。动词为 notice。
7. **overlap** [ˌəʊvəˈlæp] *v.* 重叠；与……重合
8. **stratum** [ˈstrɑːtəm] *n.* [地质] 地层；社会阶层

⑨ **stratigraphic** [strætɪˈgræfɪk] *adj.* 地层的；地层学的

⑩ **asymmetric** [ˌeɪsɪˈmetrɪk] *adj.* 不对称的；不对等的。反义词为 symmetric *adj.* 对称的

⑪ **steep** [stiːp] *adj.* （路、山等）陡峭的；（价格或要求）难以接受的，过高的；（增加或减少）急剧的，大幅度的

四、难句解析

Sitting in the middle of Hoh Xil, the mahogany colored mountain is very noticeable in the green grassland of the basin in summer, with clear and overlapping stratum visibly exposed.

① **Sitting in the middle of Hoh Xil**，现在分词作状语，修饰 mountain。

② **with clear and overlapping stratum visibly exposed**，with 接复合成分，作状语。

五、练习题

① According to the article, which statement is true about a large "red mountain" in Hoh Xil discovered by a Chinese expedition?

A. It's in Qinghai Province, Northeast China, could be dated back to the late Cretaceous or Paleogene period.

B. It is ordinary to find such large and exposed areas of red strata in China.

C. The yellowish colored mountain is very visible in the green grassland of the basin in summer.

D. It is a spectacular ancient geological antiquity.

② What does the word "mahogany" in the article mean?

A. Very beautiful.

B. Noticeable.

C. A reddish-brown color.

D. Greenish.

3 How many years ago could the red mountain be dated back to?

A. Somewhere in Northwest China's Qinghai Province.

B. Somewhere between 70 to 30 million years ago.

C. They are still trying to figure it out.

D. Before the late Cretaceous or Paleogene period.

Do your research and answer these questions orally or by writing.

1 What other geological knowledge do you have that is not in the article? Why do you think the known facts about geology are constantly changing?

2 Would you be interested in becoming a geologist? If not, why? If so, which part of the world would you like to explore and why?

Two gibbon species declared extinct in the wild in China due to excessive 'human activities'

(2022.9.7)

An assessment report on the endangered status of **primates** in China was released on Tuesday, indicating that the white-handed gibbon and northern white-cheeked gibbon have not been seen in the wild in the past few decades, meeting the **criteria** for being declared extinct in the wild.

The report was released at a conference on Tuesday, which was also the 40th anniversary of the founding of **the Endangered Species Scientific Commission of China**.

A species classified as "extinct in the wild" means that it is now found only in **captivity**, or that it needs to be released into the wild before returning to its historic areas due to habitat loss, according to the report.

The extinction of other species such as Chinese **paddlefish** and **dugongs** has reminded people that more efforts must be made to protect endangered species, experts noted.

一、背景简介

在国家濒危物种科学委员会成立 40 周年暨 2021 年度工作会议上，国家濒科委委员李保国在题为"中国灵长类动物濒危状况评估"的报告中介绍，我国分布的白掌长臂猿和北白颊长臂猿已经处于野外灭绝状态。科研人员对白掌长臂猿已知分布区及周边区适宜栖息地进行了系统调查，野外未发现有生存的种群，也未监听到其鸣叫声，有 10 年以上未有人在野外听到其鸣叫声。

引起一系列灭绝危机的直接原因主要有生态环境丧失和片段化、外来物种的侵入、资源的过度开发、环境污染、全球气候变化等。但问题根源在于人口的剧增和自然资源快速消耗、农业的不断扩张、生物资源过度利用和保护产生的惠益分配的不均衡、知识及其应用的不充分以及法律和制度的不合理等。

二、全文翻译

由于过度的"人类活动",两种长臂猿在中国宣布灭绝

周二发布的一份关于中国灵长类动物濒危状况的评估报告显示,在过去的几十年中,中国分布的白掌长臂猿、北白颊长臂猿在野外均没有被监测到,符合野外灭绝的标准。

该报告于本周二在国家濒危物种科学委员会成立40周年会议上发布。

该报告称,一个物种被归类为"野外灭绝"状态意味着其个体仅存活于圈养的环境,或者由于栖息地丧失,需经过野放后才能够回归其历史上存在的区域。

专家指出,中国白鲟和儒艮等其他物种的灭绝提醒人们,必须加大力度保护濒危物种。

三、单词点津

1. **gibbon** [ˈɡɪbən] *n.* [脊椎] 长臂猿

2. **excessive** [ɪkˈsesɪv] *adj.* 过度的,过多的。excessive consumption 超前消费

3. **primate** [ˈpraɪmeɪt] *n.* 灵长类

4. **criteria** [kraɪˈtɪərɪə] *n.* (评判或做决定的)标准,准则,尺度,是 criterion 的复数。

5. **the Endangered Species Scientific Commission of China** 国家濒危物种科学委员会

6. **captivity** [kæpˈtɪvəti] *n.* 囚禁;圈养

7 **paddlefish** ['pædlfɪʃ] *n.* 大硬鲭鱼；白鲟

8 **dugong** ['duːgɒŋ] *n.* 儒艮（一种海生哺乳动物）

四、难句解析

The extinction of other species such as Chinese paddlefish and dugongs has reminded people that more efforts must be made to protect endangered species.

1 **has reminded** 的主语是 the extinction of other species，而不是 Chinese paddlefish and dugongs，需要分清。

2 **efforts must be made** 是被动语态，这里表示强调语气。

五、练习题

1 Which statement is true to describe a species classified as "extinct in the wild"?

　A. As long as a species has not been seen in the wild for over a year.

　B. A species is totally extinct from the planet.

　C. There are fewer than 10 animals of this species in the wild.

　D. No such animal has been found in the wild over a certain period but the animal is still kept in zoos or as pets.

2 Which word does not have a similar meaning to "criteria"?

　A. Standard.

　B. Decision.

　C. Principle.

　D. Criterion.

3 According to the article, what does "the extinction of other species such as Chinese paddlefish and dugongs" remind people to do?

  A. We need to invest more in zoos to show animals to the public.

  B. We shouldn't keep pets anymore.

  C. We should pay more attention to animals on the brink of extinction.

  D. We should revive Chinese paddlefish and dugongs in the wild.

Do your research and answer these questions orally or by writing.

1 What are some of the reasons animals go extinct?

2 As human beings, what should we do to have an eco-friendly and balanced life with animals?

Breathtaking rescue fixes satellite glitch and ensures 100% success rate of China's BDS deployment

(2022.9.29)

"It was like a man standing upright when he was suddenly pushed to the left by an **external** force, and then to the right," Wang Xin, a senior engineer with the Xi'an Satellite Control Center described, as he recalled the satellite **emergency** in March 2020 where the second last satellite of the third generation of BeiDou Navigation Satellite System or the BDS-3 encountered an **abnormal** change of attitude and faced the real possibility of veering out of control.

Starting from 1994, China has sent a total of 59 BeiDou satellites into orbit in 44 space launch missions with a 100 percent success rate, and on July 31, 2020, the country announced the completion and official **commissioning** of the domestically developed mega space **infrastructure** project.

Apart from the strong performance of launch vehicles and satellites, there is a mysterious team of "star **shepherd**" behind the remarkable success, who are guarding China's largest satellite constellation to date around the clock.

Overcoming **adversity** including the COVID-19 epidemic, it was this very team that pulled off a space rescue when the BDS-3 GEO-2 satellite experienced abnormalities in March 2020 and managed to return the satellite back to its preset orbit.

一、背景简介

2020年7月31日,中国宣布全面建成北斗三号全球卫星导航系统,这是过去十年中,中国航天最为耀眼的成就之一。这项由中国自主建设、独立运行的全球卫星导航系统，在维护国家安全、服务经济社会发展方面发挥了不可替代的作用。从 1994 年北斗一号系统建设的正式启动至 2020 年北斗三号系统的全面建成，北斗卫星导航系统耗时 26 年，共组织了 44 次北斗发射任务，先后将 59 颗北斗卫星送入预定轨道，任务成功率达到 100%。

在过去的十年中，我国的在轨卫星数量越来越多，功能越来越强，价值也越来越大。作为中国太空资产最为坚实的守护者，西安卫星测控中心"牧星人"团队不辱使命，在浩瀚的宇宙中书写了更多"隐秘而伟大"的故事。

二、全文翻译

惊心动魄修复卫星故障，确保中国北斗三号全球卫星导航系统部署 100% 成功

西安卫星测控中心高级工程师王鑫说："这就好比一个人本来站姿端正，却突然出现一股外力，把这个人向左边猛推一下，又向右边猛推一下。"他回忆起 2020 年 3 月的卫星紧急情况，当时北斗三号 GEO-2 卫星出现姿态异变，面临失控可能性。

从 1994 年开始，中国共在 44 次空间发射任务中发射了 59 颗北斗卫星，成功率达到 100%。2020 年 7 月 31 日，中国宣布建成并正式启用这一国内开发的重要空间基础设施项目。

举世瞩目的成就背后，除了性能卓越的运载火箭和卫星，还有一支神秘的"牧星人"团队时刻守护着中国迄今为止规模最大的卫星系统。

在 2020 年 3 月北斗三号 GEO-2 卫星组网部署任务中，这支团队克服新冠疫情等种种不利因素，在卫星突发故障的情况下，成功将这颗卫星救回并送入预定轨道，完成了太空救援。

三、单词点津

1. **breathtaking** ['breθteɪkɪŋ] *adj.* 激动人心的，令人惊叹的
2. **BDS** 北斗卫星导航系统（英文名称：BeiDou Navigation Satellite System，简称 BDS）是中国自行研制的全球卫星导航系统，也

是继 GPS、GLONASS 之后的第三个成熟的卫星导航系统。北斗卫星导航系统（BDS）和美国 GPS、俄罗斯 GLONASS、欧盟 GALILEO，是联合国卫星导航委员会已认定的供应商。

3　**external** [ɪk'stɜːnl] *adj.* 外部的；与外国有关的。反义词 internal *adj.* 是内部的；体内的；国内的

4　**emergency** [i'mɜːdʒənsi] *n.* 突发事件；紧急情况　*adj.* 紧急情况下的；应急的

5　**abnormal** [æb'nɔːml] *adj.* 反常的，异常的。前缀 ab- 有"离开，非"之意。名词形式是 abnormality。

6　**commissioning** [kə'mɪʃənɪŋ] *n.* 试运转

7　**infrastructure** ['ɪnfrəstrʌktʃə(r)] *n.* 基础设施

8　**shepherd** ['ʃepəd] *n.* 牧羊人　*v.* 牧（羊）；带领，引领

9　**adversity** [əd'vɜːsəti] *n.* 逆境，厄运

四、难句解析

Apart from the strong performance of launch vehicles and satellites, there is a mysterious team of "star shepherd" behind the remarkable success, who are guarding China's largest satellite constellation to date around the clock.

1　**apart from**，意思是"除了……之外（本身包括在内）"，引导条件状语从句。

2　**who** 引导非限制性定语从句，修饰 team。

五、练习题

选择题

1　According to the article, what does this sentence describe——"It was like a man standing upright when he was suddenly pushed to the left by an external force, and then to the right"?

A. A man has been pushed by external force.

B. The BDS-3 encountered an abnormal change of attitude and faced the real possibility of veering out of control.

C. There is a mysterious team of "star shepherd" behind the remarkable success.

D. Humans were experiencing adversity.

2. According to the article, which action is not taken by the mysterious team of "star shepherd"?

A. It pulled off a space rescue when the BDS-3 GEO-2 satellite experienced abnormalities in March 2020.

B. It managed to return the satellite back to its preset orbit.

C. It caused the BDS-3 to encounter an abnormal change of attitude and face the real possibility of veering out of control.

D. It safeguards China's largest satellite constellation to date around the clock.

3. Which is not a synonym of "adversity" in the article?

A. Disaster.

B. Affliction.

C. Fate.

D. Hardship.

Do your research and answer these questions orally or by writing.

1. What else do you know about the BeiDou satellites and how do they impact our daily life?

2. The team has allegedly kept a 100% successful mission rate. How hard do you think it is to make something 100% successful? How can we work to make other things in life perfect?

Chinese scientists find high water content in lunar soil samples brought back by Chang'e-5 mission

(2022.9.12)

Chinese scientists' research showed the lunar soil samples brought back by the Chang'e-5 mission contain high content of water originated from solar wind.

The **formation** and **distribution** of lunar **surficial** water remains **ambiguous** despite that remote sensing data show the **prominence** of water (OH/H2O) on moon surface, due to the lack of direct evidence from sample analysis.

Latest research on the lunar soil samples brought back by the Chang'e-5 mission conducted by the scientific research team from the Institute of Geochemistry, Chinese Academy of Sciences, showed that the surface of the lunar soil samples contains high content of water **attributed** to solar wind implantation.

The results of **spectral** and **microstructural** analyses indicate that the formation and storage of solar wind-**derived** water are affected by exposure time, crystal structure, and mineral **composition** of the minerals.

一、背景简介

遥感探测发现月球表面普遍存在水（OH/H_2O），然而由于缺乏直接的样品分析证据，月表水的成因和分布一直存在争议。中国科学院地球化学研究所科研团队针对嫦娥五号带回来的月球土壤样品开展了研究，通过红外光谱和纳米离子探针分析，发现嫦娥五号矿物表层中存在大量的太阳风成因水，估算出太阳风质子注入为嫦娥五号月壤贡献的水含量至少为 170ppm。结合透射电镜与能谱分析，揭示了太阳风成因水的形成和保存主要受矿物的暴露时间、晶体结构和成分等因素影响。该研究证实了月表矿物是水的重要"储库"，为月表中纬度地区水的分布提供了重要参考。

嫦娥五号（Chang'e 5），由国家航天局组织实施研制，是中国首个实施无人月面取样返回的月球探测器。嫦娥五号的任务是中国探月工程的第六次任务，也是中国航天最复杂、难度最大的任务之一（截至 2020 年 12 月），实现了中国首次月球无人采样返回，助力月球成因和演化历史等科学研究。

二、全文翻译

中国科学家在嫦娥五号带回的月壤样品中发现高含量的水

中国科学家的研究表明，嫦娥五号任务带回的月球土壤样品含有高含量的太阳风成因水。

尽管遥感探测数据显示月表普遍存在水，但由于缺乏样品分析的直接证据，月表水的成因和分布始终存在争议。

中国科学院地球化学研究所科研团队对嫦娥五号任务月壤样品进行的最新研究表明，由于太阳风的注入，月壤样品的表面含有高含量的水。

光谱和显微结构分析结果表明，太阳风成因水的形成和储存受矿物的暴露时间、晶体结构和成分的影响。

三、单词点津

1. **formation** [fɔːˈmeɪʃn] *n.* 组成物；构成；形成；（社会、政治等的）形态

2. **distribution** [ˌdɪstrɪˈbjuːʃn] *n.* 分发；配送；（电影在各院线的）发行，上映；分配，分布

3. **surficial** [sɜːˈfɪʃəl] *adj.* 地表的；地面的

4. **ambiguous** [æmˈbɪgjuəs] *adj.* 模棱两可的，有歧义的，不确定的

5. **prominence** [ˈprɒmɪnəns] *n.* 重要，著名，突起，凸出。prominent *adj.* 突出的，显著的；杰出的，卓越的

6. **attribute** [əˈtrɪbjuːt] *v.* 把……归因于 *n.* 属性，特质；标志，象征。attribute to 归因于；归功于

7. **spectral** [ˈspektrəl] *adj.* [光]光谱的；幽灵的

8. **microstructural** [maɪkrɒˈstrʌktʃərəl] *adj.* 显微结构的

9. **derived** [dɪˈraɪvd] *adj.* 导出的；衍生的，派生的 *v.* 从……衍生出，源于；（从……中）得到。wind-derived 风驱动的

10. **composition** [ˌkɒmpəˈzɪʃn] *n.* 成分构成，成分；作品，作曲；构图

四、练习题

选择题

1. What was found in the lunar soil samples brought back by the Chang'e-5 mission?

    A. A lake was found with high water content in the lunar soil.

    B. There is an underground river with high water content in the lunar soil.

    C. The soil samples contained high water content.

    D. There was rain on the moon and it was found in lunar soils.

2. Why did the lunar soil samples contain high content of water?

    A. The results of spectral and micro-structural analyses.

    B. Solar wind implantation.

    C. The lack of direct evidence from sample analysis.

    D. The prominence of water (H_2O) on the moon's surface.

3. According to the article, which is not a factor for the formation and storage of solar wind-derived water?

   A. Exposure time.

   B. Crystal structures.

   C. Mineral composition of the minerals.

   D. Temperature of the surface.

Do your research and answer these questions orally or by writing.

1. Why is it important that we do such a detailed analysis on the surface of the moon and any water we find? What other research should we do on the moon?

2. What else do you know about Chang'e-5 mission?

Beijing distributes emotion-sensing equipment to highway and cross-province bus drivers

(2022.9.21)

A transportation company in Beijing has distributed 1,800 sets of emotion-sensing equipment to drivers to monitor their life signs and mental stress in real time in an effort to ensure driving safety.

The equipment, **initiated** by the Beijing Public Transport, was mainly given to drivers who drive on the highways or on cross-provincial long trips.

The company, in cooperation with various professional institutions, has tested more than 40,000 **operational** drivers for **psychological** suitability. The second round of testing for pilot psychological suitability has already been completed.

The emotion-sensing equipment is part of the company's efforts to strengthen driving safety for Beijing bus drivers.

Digital transformation of safety management is also being promoted by the company to improve **vehicle** safety and establish safety mechanisms.

一、背景简介

为了保证行车安全，北京公交集团以高速路、跨省运营驾驶员为重点，配发多体征情绪感知设备1,800套，实时监测驾驶员生命体征和精神压力变化。为了监督行车安全，公交集团配备专职行车安全管理人员；组建集团和分公司两级稽查中心，联同企业内部班组长、外部聘请的近百名社会交通监督员，共同承担起安全预防管理、检查监控等职责。今年，公交集团计划为部分运营车辆加装技防系统，提升安全管理数字化效率。其中，安装驾驶员异常行为识别系统 5,000 套，安装主动安全预警系统 2,000 套，这两套系统已列入新车标准配置。

二、全文翻译

北京为高速路、跨省运营驾驶员重点配发情绪感知设备

北京一家交通公司向其司机分发了 1,800 套情绪感知设备，实时监测驾驶员生命体征和精神压力变化，以确保行车安全。

该设备由北京公共交通部门配发，主要提供给高速路、跨省运营驾驶员。

该公司与相关专业机构合作，先期对 4 万余名运营驾驶员进行了心理适宜性测试。目前，已经完成第二轮驾驶员心理适宜性普测工作。

这种情绪感知设备是该公司增强北京公交车司机驾驶安全的举措之一。

该公司还正在推动安全管理的数字化转型，以提高车辆安全性并建立安全机制。

三、单词点津

① **initiate** [ɪˈnɪʃieɪt] *v.* 开始实施，发起；使了解，传授 *n.* 新加入某组织的人。initiate a meeting 发起会议

② **operational** [ˌɒpəˈreɪʃənl] *adj.* （机器、设备等）正常运转的，可使用的；运营的，业务的

③ **psychological** [ˌsaɪkəˈlɒdʒɪkl] *adj.* 心理上的，精神的；心理学的

四、难句解析

The equipment, initiated by the Beijing Public Transport, was

mainly given to drivers who drive on the highways or on cross-provincial long trips.

1. **initiated**，过去分词作定语。
2. **was given**，被动语态，主动形式为 give the equipment to drivers。
3. **who** 引导限定性定语从句，修饰 drivers。
4. **on the trips**，固定搭配，意为"在旅途中"，用介词 on。

五、练习题

选择题

1. Which of the following statements about the equipment mentioned in the article is not true?

   A. This equipment can observe the drivers' life signs and mental stress levels.

   B. The main purpose of this equipment is to reduce car accidents.

   C. This equipment can help traffic jams.

   D. This equipment can enhance driving safety.

2. Why was the equipment, initiated by the Beijing Public Transport, mainly given to drivers who drive on the highways or on cross-provincial long trips?

   A. Because these drivers' companies have connections with the Beijing Public Transport system.

   B. Because these drivers have more money and can afford the equipment.

   C. Because these drivers are more professional than city drivers.

   D. Because compared with other short distance drivers, long haul drivers are more prone to dangerous accidents.

3. Which of the following is not mentioned in the article by the Beijing Public Transport?

   A. Digital transformation of safety management.

   B. More driving safety courses.

   C. Test for psychological suitability.

   D. The emotion-sensing equipment.

Do your research and answer these questions orally or by writing.

1. How important is driving safety to human beings and why?

2. What else do you think we can do to improve driving safety?

China mulls increased penalties, employment ban on internet violators to better safeguard cybersecurity

(2022.9.15)

China's top **cyberspace** regulator on Wednesday proposed a series of **amendments** to the country's cybersecurity law including raising **penalty** and an employment ban on internet operators who violated the law to better protect the **legitimate** rights and interests of individuals and organizations in cyberspace and safeguard national security.

One of highlights of the newly introduced clauses released by the **Cyberspace Administration of China (CAC)** is the one that plans to raise the size of penalty on operators of key information infrastructure, who use **unauthorized** networking products and service, up to 10 times the amount they paid for the product or 5 percent of their previous year's **revenue**.

According to the amendments, the penalty will also be raised on internet operators who fail to stop users on their platforms from publishing information that **violates** laws and regulations or those who fail to respond to major security risks and incidents **appropriately**.

一、背景简介

《中华人民共和国网络安全法》是我国首部关于网络安全工作的基本大法，自 2017 年 6 月 1 日正式施行以来为我国网络空间安全治理提供了法律保障。为了与 2021 年相继修订和制定实施的《中华人民共和国行政处罚法》《中华人民共和国数据安全法》《中华人民共和国个人信息保护法》等法律衔接协调，2022 年，中央网信办会同相关部门起草了《关于修改〈中华人民共和国网络安全法〉的决定（征求意见稿）》。

本次修订主要针对《中华人民共和国网络安全法》中"第六章法律责任"部分条款进行了修订完善，是我国加强网络安全工作的又一有力举措，将进一步完善我国网络安全法律法规体系。

二、全文翻译

中国考虑加大处罚力度，禁止网络违法者就业，更好保护网络安全

周三，中国最高网络空间监管机构对中国网络安全法提出一系列修正案，包括对违反该法的网络运营者提高处罚和实施就业禁令，以更好地保护个人和组织在网络空间的合法权益，维护国家安全。

国家网信办发布的最新条款中的一个重点是，关键信息基础设施的运营者，若使用未经安全审查或者安全审查未通过的网络产品或者服务，将处采购金额十倍以下或者上一年度营业额百分之五以下的罚款。

根据修正案，对于未能阻止用户在其平台上发布违反法律法规的信息或未能正确处理重大安全风险和事件的网络运营者，也将加大处罚力度。

三、单词点津

1. **cyberspace** ['saɪbəspeɪs] *n.* 网络空间。cyber *adj.* （与）网络（有关）的

2. **amendment** [ə'mendmənt] *n.* 修正案；改善，（对文件或计划的）修改

3. **penalty** ['penəlti] *n.* （因违反法律、规定或合同而受到的）处罚，刑罚；（体育运动中对犯规者的）判罚，处罚

4. **legitimate** [lɪ'dʒɪtəmət] *adj.* 正当的，合理的；合法的。legitimate interests 合法权益

5. **Cyberspace Administration of China (CAC)** 中国国家互联网信息办公室。主要职责包括落实互联网信息传播方针政策和推动互联网信息传播法制建设，指导、协调、督促有关部门加强

互联网信息内容管理，依法查处违法违规网站等。

6　**unauthorized** [ʌnˈɔːθəraɪzd] *adj.* 未经许可（或批准）的，未经授权的。authorized *adj.* 经授权的；经认可的

7　**revenue** [ˈrevənjuː] *n.* （企业、组织的）收入，收益；（政府的）税收

8　**violate** [ˈvaɪəleɪt] *v.* 违反，违背，侵犯。名词形式是 violation。

9　**appropriately** [əˈprəʊprɪətli] *adv.* 适当地，恰当地

四、练习题

1　According to the article, which of the following statements is false?

　A. An employment ban was introduced on internet operators who violate the law.

　B. A series of amendments to the country's cybersecurity law will better protect the legal rights and interests of individuals and organizations in cyberspace.

　C. The CAC plans to raise the size of the penalty on operators of key information infrastructure who use illegal networking products and services.

　D. The penalty will be raised on internet users and not the operators who fail to stop users on their platforms from publishing information that violates laws and regulations.

2　What is the exact meaning of the word "revenue"?

　A. The money an individual earned from the internet.

　B. The entire amount of income before any deductions are made.

　C. The receipt you get after you buy something.

　D. The difference between this year and the previous year.

3 According to the article, what does CAC stand for?

   A. China Appropriate Cyberspace.

   B. Cyberspace Amendment of China.

   C. Cyberspace Administration of China.

   D. Cybersecurity about China.

Do your research and answer these questions orally or by writing.

1 Why do you think that China's cybersecurity law is important and how does it relate to national security?

2 What should we do when we use the internet to protect ourselves and other people? Why?

Renowned professor witnesses remarkable progress in China's higher education that is deeply rooted in Chinese spirit and culture over last decade

(2022.9.21)

A **renowned** professor of Chinese literature at Peking University shares his observation and experience on the changes **witnessed** in university education in China over the last decade, and how the sense of Chinese culture and identity have affected both young people in China and overseas over the years.

Peking University holds a key place in Chinese history as one of China's first modern national universities. The university was the base of the **New Culture Movement** as well as a **cradle** of the May 4th Movement. Its role as an **epicenter** for culture and education has greatly shaped modern China.

According to Zhang, the current education system is more rooted in the Chinese spirit and culture. In Zhang's words, "Not only have we now adopted the good aspects of the global education system, but are also more rooted in the Chinese culture. In fact, the leading role of Chinese culture is highlighted in both the teaching system and the design of the courses."

一、背景简介

党的十八大以来，党中央、国务院高度重视高等教育，习近平总书记多次就高等教育发表重要讲话、作出重要指示批示，为高等教育改革发展指明了前进的方向。

十年来，我国高等教育取得了令人瞩目的成就，建成世界最大规模的高等教育体系，整体水平进入世界第一方阵，创新创业教育领跑世界，高等教育服务国家能力显著提升。

2022 年，我国接受高等教育的人口达到 2.4 亿人，新增劳动力平均受教育年限达到 13.8 年，劳动力素质结构发生了重大变化，全民族素质得到了稳步提高。高等教育在育人方式、办学模式、管理体制、保障机制等方面不断创新，为建设世界重要人才和创新高地提供了有力支撑。

二、全文翻译

深植于中国精神文化，知名教授见证中国高等教育十年来的显著发展

北京大学中国文学系知名教授（张颐武）就过去十年间中国大学教育的变化，以及多年来中国文化和身份认同感如何影响国内外青年人分享了自己的观察和体会。

北京大学作为中国最早的近代国立大学之一，在中国历史上占据重要地位。北京大学是新文化运动的中心，也是五四运动的摇篮。它作为文化和教育的中心，对现代中国产生了极大影响。

张颐武表示，目前的教育体系更加植根于中国的精神和文化。用他的话说，"我们现在不仅采纳了全球教育体系的优点，而且更加植根于中国文化。事实上，中国文化的主导地位在教学体系和课程设计中都有所强调"。

三、单词点津

1. **renowned** [rɪ'naʊnd] *adj.* 有名望的，著名的。world-renowned 世界闻名的

2. **witness** ['wɪtnəs] *n.* （尤指犯罪或事故的）目击者；（法庭等的）证人　*v.* 目击，目睹；见证，经历

3. **New Culture Movement** 新文化运动是 20 世纪初中国一些先进知识分子发起的反对封建主义的思想解放运动，提倡民主和科学。大力提倡新道德、反对旧道德，提倡新文学，反对文言文。

4. **cradle** ['kreɪdl] *n.* 摇篮　*v.* 轻轻抱着

5. **epicenter** ['epɪsentə] *n.* [地震] 震中；中心

四、难句解析

Not only have we now adopted the good aspects of the global education system, but are also more rooted in the Chinese culture.

not only…but (also)… 在句中常用来连接两个对等的成分，also 可以省略。Not only…but (also)… 用来连接两个主语时，谓语动词的单、复数遵循"就近原则"，即和 but (also) 后的名词或代词的单、复数形式一致。not only…but (also)… 连接两个分句，当 not only 位于句首，前一个分句常用倒装来表示强调，而 but (also) 后的分句仍用陈述语序。

五、练习题

1. According to the article, which statement about Peking University is not true?

   A. Peking University is one of China's first modern universities.

   B. Peking University is partly rooted in Chinese culture and was heavily influenced by ancient Chinese emperors.

   C. Peking University was the centre of the New Culture Movement.

   D. The May 4th Movement was originated or nurtured from Peking University.

2. Which word cannot replace "renowned" in the article?

   A. Distinguished.

   B. Notable.

   C. Notorious.

   D. Well-known.

3 Which statement talking about the relationship between higher education and Chinese culture is not true?

    A. The leading role of Chinese culture is highlighted in the teaching system and the design of the courses.

    B. Chinese culture is emphasized in China's higher educational curriculum.

    C. The current education system is more rooted in the Chinese spirit and culture.

    D. The global higher education system is also rooted in Chinese culture.

Do your research and answer these questions orally or by writing.

1 According to your understanding and knowledge, what are the differences between China's and other countries' higher education? Please provide positives and negatives.

2 How do you understand the following statement—"the current education system has adopted the good aspects of the global education system, but is also more rooted in the Chinese culture"?

第 10 篇

Creativity, self-expression, flexible work culture drive Gen-Z's innovative approach to employment

(2022.8.25)

Virtual avatar creators, pet-food chefs, cat **morticians**, drone pilots, wardrobe organizers...All these unfamiliar but appealing-sounding and innovative jobs **spawned** by new market demand are now increasingly becoming dream jobs for China's youngest adults.

As China's Generation-Z—those born between the late 1990s and early 2010s—is emerging as the main labor force and consumers, their dream jobs have redefined traditional employment ideas.

New social trends and demands—such as young people's **enthusiasm** for virtual **consumption** and digital products—have given rise to **niche** jobs amid the government's encouragement of **diversified** economic development.

The emergence of new occupations has **stimulated** the job market, meeting consumers' creative demand for services and injecting new vitality into economic and social development, experts said, while appealing for a strengthened regulation of **unprecedented** factors.

一、背景简介

Z 世代（Gen-Z）是美国及欧洲的流行用语，意指在 1995—2009 年出生的人，又称网络世代、互联网世代，统指受到互联网、即时通信、短讯、MP3、智能手机和平板电脑等科技产物影响很大的一代人。

在中国，Z 世代按时间角度可定义为 1995—2009 年出生的人群，即"95

后"和"00后"。据 2021 年国内统计数据显示,中国 Z 世代人群约占 2.6 亿人,撑起了 4 万亿的消费市场,开销占全国家庭总开支的 13%,消费增速远超其他年龄层。同时,中国移动互联网 Z 世代活跃设备数近 3.25 亿,相比起 2016 年同期的 1.66 亿,5 年时间规模增长近乎翻倍,Z 世代已成长为移动互联网网民中的新势力。

二、全文翻译

创造力、自我表达、灵活的工作文化推动 Z 世代的创新就业方式

虚拟头像制作者、宠物食品厨师、猫咪殡葬师、无人机操作员、衣柜收纳师……这些新型职业由新的市场需求催生,不为人熟知,听起来却很有意思,正日益成为中国年轻人的理想职业。

随着 20 世纪 90 年代末至 21 世纪 10 年代初出生的中国"Z 世代"逐渐成为主要劳动力和消费者,他们的理想职业重新定义了传统的就业观念。

在政府鼓励多样化经济发展的同时,新的社会趋势和需求,例如年轻人对虚拟消费和数字产品的热情,催生了利基工作。

专家表示,新兴职业的出现刺激了就业市场,满足了消费者对服务的创新性需求,为经济和社会发展注入了新的活力。同时,专家也呼吁加强对新情况的监管。

三、单词点津

1. **virtual** ['vɜːtʃuəl] *adj.* (在计算机或互联网上存在或出现的)虚拟的,模拟的。VR(Virtual Reality)虚拟现实技术

2. **avatar** ['ævətɑː(r)] *n.* (人或思想的)化身,体现;(在电脑游戏或网络中代表使用者的)图标,头像。电影《阿凡达》的英文名也是这个单词。

3. **mortician** [mɔːˈtɪʃn] *n.* 殡葬业者

4. **spawn** [spɔːn] *v.* 引发,促生;大量生产;产卵 *n.* (鱼、青蛙、

软体动物、甲壳类等的）卵

5. **enthusiasm** [ɪnˈθjuːziæzəm] *n.* 热情，热忱；热爱的事物。形容词形式是 enthusiastic。

6. **consumption** [kənˈsʌmpʃn] *n.* 消费，消耗；食用。fuel consumption 油耗

7. **niche** [niːʃ] *adj.* 利基，（产品）针对特定小群体的。利基指针对企业的优势细分出来的市场，这个市场不大，而且没有提供令人满意的服务。如果有针对性、专业性很强的产品推进这个市场，则有盈利的基础。

8. **diversified** [daɪˈvɜːsɪfaɪd] *adj.* 多样化的；各种的

9. **stimulate** [ˈstɪmjuleɪt] *v.* 促进，激发（某事物）；使（身体，生物系统）兴奋

10. **unprecedented** [ʌnˈpresɪdentɪd] *adj.* 前所未有的，史无前例的

四、练习题

1. Which of the following jobs is not a dream job for China's youngest adults?

   A. Pet-food chefs.

   B. Virtual Avatar Creators.

   C. Drone Pilots.

   D. Taxi Drivers.

2. According to the article, which of the following statements is not true?

   A. The new occupations have come about due to demand by consumers.

B. The young people's interest in virtual consumption and digital products has given rise to new occupations.

C. The younger generation's dream jobs have redefined and replaced traditional employment ideas.

D. The new occupations are described as unfamiliar but appealing and innovative.

3. Which can not replace "unprecedented" in the article?

A. Never done before.

B. Original.

C. Unique.

D. Wonderful.

Do your research and answer these questions orally or by writing.

1. What is your dream job? Why?

2. What new jobs do you believe will be created for future demand?

Revealing a confident, vigorous and real China via window of short videos on rural life

(2022.8.4)

  The popularity of small-town and rural bloggers online across China's short-format video platforms are **blazing the trail** in new trends across China, and revealed a true, diverse, and dynamic Chinese society.

  As the most popular short-format video platforms, Kuaishou and Douyin continue to offer windows into China's rural life. Rural bloggers are becoming increasingly comfortable in using their smartphones to **showcase** their ordinary yet colorful lives and diverse values to netizens around the world. It is also a convenient way for young Chinese **urbanites** to **indulge** in a yearning for a less stressful, **vibrant** rural life amid the narrowing gap in living standards between urban and rural areas.

  Videos showing **authentic** rural lives remain highly popular across **numerous** social media platforms. Technological advancements have made the sharing of **ordinary** people's lives easier and far more realistic, while showing others how rural daily life is really like, which is worth recording to inspire others, Zhang Yiwu, a Peking University professor, told the *Global Times*.

一、背景简介

  2022 年 5 月，中共中央办公厅、国务院办公厅印发《乡村建设行动实施方案》，提出要推进数字技术与农村生产生活深度融合，持续开展数字乡村试点。农村题材短视频以独特的视听体验、符号化的情感连接、短平快传播等特点，一度成为流量热点。短视频是互联网时代一种新的展现形式和传播方式，乡村生活类短视频在展现、传承乡村文化中有着积极意义。业界和学界应该探索一条可持续发展的策略，立足乡村现实生活，加强城乡之间的社会、文化、经济联系，传播乡村文化、展现脱贫攻坚伟大成就。

二、全文翻译

通过乡村生活短视频展示自信、活力和真实的中国

小镇和乡村题材短视频在短视频平台上的流行正在引领中国新趋势，展示了真实、多元和充满活力的社会图景。

快手和抖音作为最受欢迎的短视频平台，依然是外界了解中国乡村生活的窗口。乡村短视频创作者越来越乐于通过手机向世界各地的网民展示他们平凡而丰富的生活和多样化的价值观。随着城乡生活水平差距不断缩小，在城市居住的中国年轻人也用这种便捷方式憧憬着压力较小、充满活力的乡村生活。

展示真实乡村生活的视频在众多社交媒体平台上依然非常受欢迎。北京大学教授张颐武在接受《环球时报》采访时表示，科技进步让人们分享自己的生活变得更简单，也更加实事求是，向外界展示了乡村日常生活的真实情况，这值得记录下来，启发更多的人。

三、单词点津

1. **blaze the trail** 开辟道路，引领
2. **showcase** ['ʃəʊkeɪs] *n.* 展示（本领、优点等）的场合；玻璃陈列柜 *v.* 展示，展现
3. **urbanite** ['ɜːbənaɪt] *n.* 都市人
4. **indulge** [ɪn'dʌldʒ] *v.* 沉湎，沉溺；纵容；参加（尤指违法活动）。indulge in 沉溺于
5. **vibrant** ['vaɪbrənt] *adj.* 充满活力的；醒目的；强劲的
6. **authentic** [ɔː'θentɪk] *adj.* 真实的；逼真的；可靠的

7 **numerous** ['nju:mərəs] *adj.* 众多的，许多的

8 **ordinary** ['ɔ:dɪnəri] *adj.* 普通的，平淡无奇的，平庸的。the ordinary 常见的人（或事物）

四、难句解析

难句

Technological advancements have made the sharing of ordinary people's lives easier and far more realistic, while showing others how rural daily life is really like, which is worth recording to inspire others.

1 **realistic** 的比较级是 more realistic。

2 **which** 引导非限定性定语从句，修饰前面的句子。

3 **worth doing**，意为"值得做某事"。

五、练习题

选择题

1 According to the article, which statement is not true?

  A. Rural bloggers become better at using their smartphones to showcase their ordinary yet colorful lives.

  B. The short-format videos show how rural daily life can be and are helpful in inspiring others.

  C. Sharing of ordinary people's lives comes to reality by technological advancements.

  D. Only the small-town and rural bloggers reveal a true, diverse, and dynamic Chinese society through short-format video platforms.

2 Which word cannot replace "indulge" in the article?

  A. immerse.

  B. Satisfy.

C. Gratify.

D. Abstain.

3. What do short-format video bloggers use in order to share their videos?

A. Cellphones.

B. Internet.

C. Video editing software.

D. All of the above.

Do your research and answer these questions orally or by writing.

1. Do you like to use your smartphone to showcase your life? If so, how can you make your short videos more attractive to audiences? If not, why?

2. What type of videos do you prefer and why? If you don't like videos, what type of entertainment do you like?

Behind a trending 'green horse' plushie produced by a Chinese museum was design team wanting to narrow distance between cultural relics and the younger generation

(2022.9.5)

This past summer, a pea-colored, BoJack-look museum-produced horse **plushie** went viral on the Chinese internet.

The "green horse" featuring a national-treasure bronze horse **statue** of the Eastern Han Dynasty (25-220 AD), has not only become a new star in the already competitive museum cultural products market in China, but also managed to connect different versions of cultural heritage with young Chinese people, according to the head of the design team at the Gansu Provincial Museum in Northwest China.

Recently, as a follow-up product, a Lego-style brick toy of the bronze horse was also released by the Gansu museum, attracting young people's attention.

According to data from the **National Cultural Heritage Administration**, more than 124,000 types of cultural and creative products were developed in museums across the country in 2020, generating an actual revenue of over 1.1 billion yuan ($160 million).

一、背景简介

甘肃省博物馆的"镇馆之宝"——铜奔马,又称"马踏飞燕",20世纪60年代出土于甘肃省武威市雷台汉墓,1983年被确定为中国旅游标志。

铜奔马造型奇特,矫健优美,如在空中飞驰,一足超掠飞鸟,表现了中国古代艺术匠师丰富的想象力和高超的铸造工艺。近年来,甘肃省博物馆推出以铜奔马为主题的系列文创产品,让文物走进生活,受到人们的喜爱。

二、全文翻译

中国某博物馆推出的"绿马"玩偶走红的背后,蕴含着设计团队拉近文物与年轻一代距离的希望

2022年夏天,一个豌豆色、波杰克风格、由博物馆推出的毛绒马玩具在网上走红。

中国西北部甘肃省博物馆文创团队负责人表示,以东汉(公元25—公元220年)国宝铜奔马为原型的"绿马"不仅成为中国博物馆文创市场的激烈竞争中一颗冉冉升起的新星,还成功地让不同版本的文物贴近了中国年轻人。

最近,甘肃博物馆还推出了一款铜奔马的乐高风格玩具作为后续产品,吸引了年轻人的注意。

根据国家文物局的数据,2020年,全国的博物馆共开发了12.4万余种文创产品,实际收入超过11亿元人民币(约1.6亿美元)。

三、单词点津

1. **plushie** [plʌʃi] *n.* 毛绒玩具
2. **statue** ['stætʃuː] *n.* (石或金属做的动物或人的)雕像
3. **National Cultural Heritage Administration** 国家文物局

四、练习题

1. According to the article, which of the following statements is incorrect?

   A. The pea-colored, BoJack-look horse plushie, is a cultural relic.

   B. The cultural and creative products developed in museums across the country in 2020 were very profitable.

C. Museum-created cultural and creative products are not all the exact copies of the cultural relics.

D. A museum-produced Lego-style brick toy of the bronze horse also became very popular.

2 According to the article, why do museums like to design and produce cultural and creative products?

A. In order to attract more young people.

B. To earn more money for the museums.

C. Because the museum staff are inspired by the cultural relics for designing purposes.

D. With the desire to bring cultural relics closer to the younger generation.

3 Which word can not replace "generate" in the article?

A. Produce.

B. Create.

C. Originate.

D. Settle.

Do your research and answer these questions orally or by writing.

1 Which museum have you been to that you liked the most and why? Which museum would you like to visit someday?

2 Did you hear about the creative products from museums before reading this article? What do you think about them?

More young people in China are seeking a career in rural areas and local communities, bringing with them knowledge, vitality

(2022.6.16)

The number of college graduates in 2022 is expected to be 10.76 million, an increase of 1.67 million year-on-year, making a new record in both scale and growth. However, against the **backdrop** of the COVID-19 epidemic, graduates are likely to face challenges in the job market. It has been predicted that this summer could be the "hardest employment season."

At the same time, Chinese society has entered a new stage of development, with trends in employment also shifting. Staying in big cities, returning their homes, choosing to occupy **grass-roots** positions, starting their own businesses, or the **evolution** of new jobs, nowadays, Gen-Zers in China are presented with a wide range of innovative and diverse opportunities.

More young people have **flocked** to less-developed regions in China to start their careers in villages or grass-roots communities in recent years, making them a new workforce in the rural **revitalization** process.

Luckily, the guidance and support provided by the government toward grass-roots employment have increased, and so has related learning in colleges and universities, which have allowed college graduates to better achieve their career and life goals in grass-roots positions.

一、背景简介

就业是最大的民生。2022年，高校毕业生首次突破千万，规模和增量均创历史新高，千方百计开拓大学生就业岗位成了保就业的重中之重。2022年6月，多部门联合下发了《关于做好2022年普通高校毕业生到城乡社区就业工作的通知》，其中明确提出，多渠道吸纳高校毕业生到城乡社区就业创业，为提高城乡社区治理和服务精准化精细化水平、推进基层治理体系和治理能力现代化建设提供人才支撑。

当前的中国城乡社区正在经历深刻变革，早已不是落后和闭塞的代名词。快递进村、网络入户，农村基本公共服务体系逐渐提升；教育、医疗等社会保障待遇的城乡差距不断缩小；特色城镇建设和县域经济发展催生了新业态，形成了特色产业。这些变化也使得大学毕业生到基层就业不仅有机遇有岗位，也具备了越来越完备的基础条件。基层治理、乡村振兴呼唤人才，同时也必然是造就人才的舞台。

二、全文翻译

越来越多的中国青年怀揣知识与热情在乡村和社区街道就业

2022年高校毕业生人数预计为1,076万人，同比增长167万人，规模和增量均创历史纪录。然而，在新冠疫情背景下，毕业生可能面临就业难的问题。据预测，今年夏天可能是"最难就业季"。

与此同时，中国进入了一个新的社会发展阶段，就业趋势也发生了变化。如今，中国的"Z世代"面临着创新和多元的机会——他们可以留在大城市，返乡，下基层工作，创业，或探索新的职业。

近年来，越来越多的年轻人涌向中国欠发达地区，在农村或基层社区开始职业生涯，成为乡村振兴进程中的生力军。

幸运的是，政府加大了对基层就业的指导和支持，高校也增加了相关课程，大学毕业生能够更好地在基层岗位上实现职业发展和生活目标。

三、单词点津

1. **backdrop** ['bækdrɒp] *n.* （舞台的）背景幕布，（事件的）背景
2. **grass-roots** ['grɑːsˈruːts] *n.* （组织、运动的）基层
3. **evolution** [ˌiːvəˈluːʃn] *n.* 进化（论）；演变，发展
4. **flock** [flɒk] *v.* 聚集，成群而行
5. **revitalization** [ˌriːˌvaɪtəlaɪˈzeɪʃn] *n.* 复兴，复苏。rural vitalization 乡村振兴

四、难句解析

难句

More young people have flocked to less-developed regions in China to start their careers in villages or grass-roots communities in recent years, making them a new workforce in the rural revitalization process.

1. **less-developed**，"副词+过去分词"的结构，作定语，意为"欠发达的"。
2. **making them...** 现在分词作非谓语动词，是对前一句话的补充。
3. **in the process**，注意介词用 in，意为"在……过程中"。

五、练习题

选择题

1. According to the article, what is not mentioned as a new trend?
   A. Staying in big cities.
   B. Returning to hometowns.
   C. Choosing to take grass-roots positions.
   D. Continuing higher education.

2. Which reason is not in the article as being responsible for the "hardest employment season"?

   A. The number of college graduates in 2022 is expected to be 10.76 million.

   B. The COVID-19 epidemic.

   C. Universities don't hold job fairs anymore.

   D. Trends in employment are shifting.

3. Which of the following statements is not right about grass-roots employment?

   A. Grass-roots employment means working with vegetables.

   B. Grass-roots employment could mean lower-paying jobs.

   C. Grass-roots employment means low-level work.

   D. Grass-roots employment means organizations at a lower level.

Do your research and answer these questions orally or by writing.

1. In such a competitive job market, if you cannot find your dream job, what else would you like to do?

2. What can you do in order to better prepare yourself for a competitive job market?

第三部分 Culture

第1篇

Chinese artists keep tradition alive with database of decorative patterns

(2022.8.23)

Almost everything in the nature, like clouds, flowers and sea waves, or even things that do not exist in reality such as **mythical** dragons, phoenixes and qilin (Chinese unicorn) inspired the **ancestors** of today's Chinese to create diverse **decorative** patterns on objects ranging from daily life **necessities** to pure artworks.

They do not just depict traditional Chinese **aesthetics** and **wordlessly** record the essence of people's lives, but also highlight exchanges between China and other regions. They have also attracted foreigners such as British architect Owen Jones, who depicted Chinese **ornaments** in a 19th century book.

The huge number of these decorations increases the difficulty of **conservation** efforts. Fortunately, many Chinese artists have been considering various ways to pass down this culture to the next generation.

Huang Qingsui, a Zhuang ethnic art designer, numbers among these artists. He started collecting decorative patterns from rural areas in 2013 and recorded them in an online database that now contains more than 20,000 traditional decorations.

一、背景简介

少数民族纹样寓意吉祥、美好，来源于生活又高于生活，不同于实物的写实，令织锦纹样更抽象，但每一个纹样背后所承载的细腻和饱满，传达了各民族的审美情趣和民族信仰。各民族文化背景不同，相同纹样被赋予不同的含义，当地妇女将生活中的点滴美好和对美好生活的期盼以丝绸、布帛等为媒介，用纹样的形式记录下来，使其得以流传。本文介绍了设计师们挖掘整理中国纹样，建设中国传统纹样数据库的故事。

二、全文翻译

中国艺术家建立装饰纹样数据库，让传统纹样重焕生机

自然界中几乎所有事物，比如云、花和海浪，甚至是现实中不存在的东西，比如神话中的龙、凤和麒麟，都启发了我们的祖先在各种物品——从日常生活必需品到纯艺术品——上面创造不同的装饰纹样。

这些装饰纹样不仅展示了中国传统美学，无声地记录了人们的真实生活，还增进了中国与其他地区的交流。纹样也吸引了外国人，比如英国建筑师欧文·琼斯（Owen Jones），他在19世纪的一本书中描绘了中国的装饰品。

装饰纹样数量庞大，为其保护工作增添了不少难度。幸运的是，许多中国艺术家一直在思考通过各种方式将这种文化传承给下一代。

身为艺术设计师的壮族小伙黄清穗就是这些艺术家中的一员。2013年，他开始收集乡村地区的装饰纹样，并将其录入线上数据库中，该数据库目前收录了2万多种传统装饰纹样。

三、单词点津

1. **mythical** [ˈmɪθɪkl] *adj.* 神话中的，想象的，虚构的。名词形式为 myth，意为"神话，虚构的人（事）"。

2. **ancestor** [ˈænsestə(r)] *n.* [生物] 祖先

3. **decorative** [ˈdekərətɪv] *adj.* 装饰性的，用作装饰的

4. **necessity** [nəˈsesəti] *n.* 必需品

5. **aesthetics** [iːsˈθetɪks] *n.* 美学；美学理论；艺术美。注意本词本身就有字母 s。形容词形式为 aesthetic，意为"美的；美学的；具有审美趣味的"。

6. **wordlessly** [ˈwɜːdlɪslɪ] *adv.* 无言地

7. **ornament** [ˈɔːnəmənt] *n.* 装饰品

8. **conservation** [ˌkɒnsəˈveɪʃn] *n.* 保护，保存；节约。动词形式为 conserve，意为"保存"。

四、难句解析

Fortunately, many Chinese artists have been considering various ways to pass down this culture to the next generation.

1. **have been considering** 是现在完成进行时，这是英语中动词的一种基本时态，其构成为：主语＋助动词（have/has）＋been＋动词的现在分词＋其他成分。表示动作从过去某一时间开始，一直持续到现在，或者刚刚终止，或者可能仍然要继续下去。

2. **pass down sth. to**，意为"把……传承下去"。

五、练习题

1. According to the article, which statement is incorrect?

    A. The decorative patterns portray traditional Chinese aesthetics and record people's lives.

    B. The diverse and decorative patterns stem from our ancestors.

    C. The diverse and decorative patterns are applied on objects ranging from daily life necessities to pure artworks.

    D. The ancestors of today's Chinese created diverse and decorative patterns exclusively based on nature such as clouds, flowers, and sea waves.

2. About the conservation work of the decorative patterns, which statement is not mentioned in the article?

   A. An online database has been created and now more than 20,000 traditional decorations have been stored.

   B. The Chinese decorative patterns attracted worldwide attention and everyone studied and wrote books about them, such as British architect Owen Jones, who depicted Chinese ornaments in a 19th century book.

   C. A Zhuang ethnic art designer has been collecting decorative patterns from rural areas since 2013.

   D. A lot of Chinese artists have been putting in efforts to pass down this culture to the next generation.

3. Which word below is not a synonym of "conservation"?

   A. Protection.

   B. Preservation.

   C. Safeguarding.

   D. Clearance.

Do your research and answer these questions orally or by writing.

1. Do you like to use decorative patterns in your home? Where are they and which style do you like?

2. In terms of passing on the decorative patterns to the younger generation, what would you suggest the Chinese artists to do?

第三部分 文化

Guizhou Province holds ethnic art festival to promote local intangible culture

(2022.8.23)

After the opening ceremony was held on Thursday at the 200-year-old two-story Lianghu Club in Liping county, 20 artists and **architects** along with 200 culture experts set off on a three-day field trip, while a folk music concert was held on Sunday.

In 2015, many of the villages in the **prefecture** were finally connected by paved roads. Through the government's poverty **alleviation** efforts, more and more artists have traveled to this area to help boost the ethnic groups' cultural development since the last county was lifted out of extreme poverty in 2020.

Zidang village is the cradle of ethnic **Dong folk songs**, a World Intangible Cultural Heritage. Now **influential** cross-disciplinary artists are **reinterpreting** this cultural heritage in a modern way.

一、背景简介

贵州是非物质文化遗产大省，现有国家级非物质文化遗产名录85项（140处）、省级561项（653处），数量位居全国前列。

侗族大歌是在中国侗族地区一种多声部、无指挥、无伴奏、自然和声的民间合唱形式，也是侗族人民在社会实践活动中创造出来的优秀民族文化成果之一。它起源于春秋战国时期，至今已有2,500多年的历史。

二、全文翻译

贵州省举办民族艺术节，弘扬地方非物质文化

黎平县两层楼高的两湖会馆有着200年的历史，周四在此举办的艺

术节开幕式结束后,20 名艺术家和建筑师以及 200 名文化学者开始了为期三天的实地考察,并在周日举办了一场民间音乐会。

2015 年,该地区的许多村庄通过条条大道连接起来。自最后一个贫困县于 2020 年脱贫以来,越来越多的艺术家在政府脱贫攻坚的努力下前往该地,帮助推动少数民族文化发展。

自当村是世界非物质文化遗产侗族民歌的发源地。现在,有影响力的多领域艺术家们正在以现代方式重新诠释这一文化遗产。

三、单词点津

1. **architect** ['ɑ:kɪtekt] *n.* 建筑师,设计师
2. **prefecture** ['pri:fektʃə(r)] *n.* 辖区;省;县。autonomous prefecture 自治州
3. **alleviation** [ə,li:vɪ'eɪʃn] *n.* 减轻,缓和
4. **Dong folk songs** 侗族民歌
5. **influential** [,ɪnflu'enʃl] *adj.* 有影响力的;有势力的
6. **reinterpret** [,ri:ɪn'tɜ:prɪt] *v.* 重新解释

四、难句解析

Through the government's poverty alleviation efforts, more and more artists have traveled to this area to help boost the ethnic groups' cultural development since the last county was lifted out of extreme poverty in 2020.

1. **poverty alleviation**,意为"扶贫"。
2. **was lifted out of extreme poverty**,被动语态,意为"被帮扶脱贫"。
3. **since** 表示"自从……以来",一般用于完成时。

五、练习题

1. According to the article, which statement is true?

   A. At a two-week ethnic art festival in Southeast China's Guizhou Province, 200 cultural experts including 20 artists and architects set off on a three-day field trip.

   B. Since the last county was lifted out of extreme poverty in 2020, the ethnic groups' cultural development has started to boost.

   C. Prior to the government putting in the poverty alleviation efforts, more and more artists have traveled to this area to help boost the ethnic groups' cultural development.

   D. A folk music concert, as the opening ceremony, was held on Thursday at the 200-year-old two-story Lianghu Club in Liping county.

2. Which is not a factor for the ethnic groups' cultural development starting to boost?

   A. The ethnic Dong folk songs is a World Intangible Cultural Heritage.

   B. The ethnic art festival is being held in this area.

   C. Nowadays, villages in this area are connected by established roads.

   D. Powerful cross-disciplinary artists are reinterpreting this cultural heritage in a modern way.

3. Which is not a synonym of "alleviation"?

   A. Mitigate.

   B. Diminution.

   C. Raise.

   D. Abate.

Do your research and answer these questions orally or by writing.

1. Why do we need to keep and promote remote ethnic local culture?
2. When we promote local culture, why do we need to bring in outside artists, architects and culture experts?

Ruins site spanning Neolithic age to Qing Dynasty discovered in East China

(2022.9.22)

A large ruins site was recently discovered in Suzhou, East China's Jiangsu Province, which **spans from** the Neolithic age to Qing Dynasty (1644-1911) and 700 cultural relics have been **unearthed** so far.

The ruins site, called Tangbei ruins, has a large area and a long time span. It is seen as having great **significance** for understanding the historical context of the origin, formation and development of the civilization in Suzhou and the process of the **integration** of the region into the **pluralistic** and integrated pattern of Chinese civilization, Jiangsu TV reported.

According to the report, the site covers an area of around 200,000 square meters. When archeological researchers **excavated** the ruins, they found remains of wells, paddy fields and tombs.

Around 700 cultural relics have been unearthed, including a painted pottery pot discovered in a well. The pot is black with several red lines and is **exquisitely** painted.

一、背景简介

塘北遗址为新发现的一处新石器时代至清代大型遗址，位于吴中区郭巷街道，面积约 20 万平方米，是一处从崧泽文化晚期一直延续至今的长时段大型遗址，目前发掘面积共计 1,100 平方米。遗址文化堆积丰富，最厚处达 2 米，地层分 10 层，分崧泽、良渚、马桥、春秋、汉、明清 6 个时期。此次发掘清理遗迹单位 630 处，出土文物 700 多件（组），填补了苏州地域文明探源多处空白，为研究良渚至商周时期文化及社会发展提供了丰富的考古资料。

二、全文翻译

中国东部发现新石器时代至清代大型遗址

近日，中国东部江苏省苏州市发现一处大型遗址，该遗址时间横跨新石器时代至清代，迄今已出土700件文物。

该遗址被称为塘北遗址，面积大，时间跨度长。据江苏电视台报道，该处遗址对了解苏州文明的起源、形成和发展史，以及该地区融入多元一体的中华文明格局的进程具有重要意义。

据报道，该遗址占地约20万平方米。考古学家在发掘遗址时，发现了水井、稻田和墓葬的遗迹。

大约有700件文物出土，其中包括在一口井中发现的漆陶壶。该壶为黑色，饰有几条红线，画风精致。

三、单词点津

1. **span from...to...** 接时间，表示跨越的时间长度。
2. **unearth** [ʌn'ɜːθ] *v.* 发掘，使出土；发现，揭露
3. **significance** [sɪɡ'nɪfɪkəns] *n.* 重要性，意义；含义
4. **integration** [ˌɪntɪ'ɡreɪʃn] *n.* 结合；融合
5. **pluralistic** [ˌplʊərə'lɪstɪk] *adj.* 多元化的
6. **excavate** ['ekskəveɪt] *v.* 挖掘（古物）；挖（洞），开凿
7. **exquisitely** [ek'skwɪzɪtli] *adv.* 精致地，精巧地；敏锐地

四、练习题

1. According to the article, which statement it incorrect?

   A. The ruins can help us learn more about the historical context of civilization in Suzhou, including its origin, formation and development.

B. The remains of wells, paddy fields and tombs have been unearthed in the ruins.

C. The Tangbei ruins is seen as having great significance for understanding the historical context in Suzhou.

D. The Tangbei ruins keep the region isolated from the pluralistic and integrated pattern of Chinese civilization.

2. Which object is not mentioned as one of the unearthed items in the Tangbei ruins?

A. A black roughly painted pottery pot with several red lines.

B. Wells and paddy fields.

C. Rice field and graves.

D. 700 cultural relics.

3. Which usage of "excavate" is wrong?

A. They have a licence to excavate the mine.

B. The mining company is excavating the oil site.

C. Good teachers always like to excavate the students' brains.

D. Many researchers are reaching the relics excavated from the tombs.

Do your research and answer these questions orally or by writing.

1. When we find a new ruin, should we unearth the relics or keep them in the ground to better protect them?

2. Have you observed any relics and what impression did you get from them?

Never-before-seen bronze beast with four wings found at Sanxingdui Ruins

(2022.8.16)

Archaeologists found a **mythical** beast with four wings during the most recent excavation of the Sanxingdui Ruins in Sichuan Province, the Xinhua News Agency reported on Monday.

This is the first time such an unusual mythical beast **bronze** has been found at the **archaeological** site.

The little mythical beast was found on the top of a bronze statue in Pit No.8. The four-winged mythical beast has a round tiger-like head with sharp teeth and carries a **sacred** tree on its back.

The beast is seen with a sacred tree on the back, a "different state of mind the ancient Shu people have at the time," as archaeologists **speculated**. The mythical beast is said also may have multiple functions.

Moreover, a pig-nose dragon bronze ware was also found during the most recent excavation, where archaeologists speculate that the bronze may have been a special **decoration** for a building.

一、背景简介

1986 年,三星堆首度发掘,青铜大立人、青铜神树、青铜大面具、黄金权杖等众多从未见过的文物器型,从 1 号坑和 2 号坑出土。2019 年 10 月到 2020 年 10 月,三星堆 6 个新祭祀坑先后被找到,并陆续启动发掘。在三星堆遗址祭祀区考古工作接近尾声的时候,考古队员在 8 号坑中又新发现了一件"四翼小神兽",这是三星堆发现的第一件带翅膀的神兽。据介绍,"四翼小神兽"发现于 8 号坑的一件铜尊器盖顶部,该器盖位于 8 号坑的中间区域,被暂命名为镂空立兽器盖。四翼神兽或许是古蜀人对真实动物的抽象再造,也是多种动物的混合体。这件极富想象力的镂空立兽器盖，直观地显示出古蜀人对青铜尊这一祭祀礼器特有的理解和使用方式，进一步为中华文明多元一体的格局提供生动例证。

二、全文翻译

三星堆遗址发现首件四翼青铜兽

据新华社周一报道，考古学家在四川省三星堆遗址的最新考古工作中发现了一只有四只翅膀的神兽。

这是第一次在考古遗址中发现如此不同寻常的青铜神兽。

这只小神兽是在8号坑的一件铜尊器盖的顶部发现的。这只四翼神兽脑袋圆润类似老虎，还有一口锋利的牙齿，背上有一棵神树。

考古学家推测，这头神兽背上的神树，展现了古蜀人不同的精神境界。神兽或许也具有多种功能。

此外，在最近的发掘中还发现了一件猪鼻龙形青铜器，考古学家推测这件青铜器可能是建筑的特殊装饰。

三、单词点津

1. **mythical** [ˈmɪθɪkl] *adj.* 神话的，神话中的；想象的，虚构的
2. **bronze** [brɒnz] *n.* 青铜；青铜色　*adj.* 青铜制的；青铜色的
3. **archaeological** [ˌɑːkɪəˈlɒdʒɪkəl] *adj.* 考古学的；考古的
4. **sacred** [ˈseɪkrɪd] *adj.* 神的；神圣的；宗教的
5. **speculate** [ˈspekjuleɪt] *v.* 猜测，推测；投机。speculate on sth. 考虑某事
6. **decoration** [ˌdekəˈreɪʃn] *n.* 装饰；装饰品

四、难句解析

Moreover, a pig-nose dragon bronze ware was also found during the most recent excavation, where archaeologists speculate that the bronze may have been a special decoration for a building.

1. **was found**，被动语态，find 的过去分词是 found。

② **where** 引导的从句修饰主句的谓语动词，作地点状语，与前面连起来就是 a bronze ware was found where archaeologists…。

五、练习题

1. According to the article, which statement is true?

    A. Archaeologists found a factual beast with four wings during the most up to date excavation of the Sanxingdui Ruins.

    B. The four-winged mythical beast has a round tiger-like head and is perched on a sacred tree.

    C. The mythical beast is affirmed to have multiple functions.

    D. The archaeologists guess that the pig-nose dragon bronze may have been a special ornament for a building.

2. According to the article, what does it mean that the mind of the ancient Shu people was different at the time?

    A. Ancient Shu people have different thinking styles.

    B. Shu people are different from human beings.

    C. Shu people are abnormal.

    D. Shu people have different views at various stages.

3. Which word below is not a synonym of "sacred"?

    A. Spiritual.

    B. Religious.

    C. Believable.

    D. Blessed.

Do your research and answer these questions orally or by writing.

1. What can we learn from ruins and relics?

2. Have you seen any relics? Which one was the most impressive and why?

Chinese animation 100

(2022.9.19)

Debuting on August 3, 2005, *Pleasant Goat and Big Big Wolf* is a Chinese animated television **series** created by Huang Weiming and produced by Creative Power Entertaining. With more than 2,000 episodes and 10 films, the *Pleasant Goat and Big Big Wolf* **franchise** is hugely popular in China.

The show centers on a group of goats living in Goat Village of Green Green Grassland. Weslie, one of the main characters, is a goat who wears a blue **ribbon** with a bell around his neck. Smart and optimistic, he always comes up with good ideas to help others and save the goats from getting eaten by Wolffy. His goat friends include the lazy Paddi, the beautiful Tibbi, the strong Sparky and the thoughtful Jonie.

One of the most successful Chinese **animated** television series, the show has been broadcast on over 75 cable and satellite television stations in China. It has also been aired in more than 100 countries including India, South Korea, Malaysia, Singapore, Indonesia, Cambodia and North America.

一、背景简介

中国动画（Chinese Animation）起源于20世纪20年代，1922年摄制了中国第一部动画《舒振东华文打字机》，揭开了中国动画史的一页。直至20世纪40年代，万氏兄弟创作了中国第一部长篇动画《铁扇公主》，发行到东南亚和日本地区，并受到人们的热烈欢迎，为中国动画走向国际作了好的铺垫。综观中国动画这几十年的发展，可以看到中国动画始终致力于一条本国特色的道路,在改革开放以后,在世界动画的大潮中也未放弃这一宗旨。

二、全文翻译

中国动画 100 年

《喜羊羊与灰太狼》于 2005 年 8 月 3 日首播,这是一部由黄伟明创作、原创动力文化传播有限公司制作的动画电视连续剧。《喜羊羊与灰太狼》系列有 2,000 多集和 10 部电影,在中国非常受欢迎。

该片聚焦于一群生活在青青草原的羊。主角喜羊羊是一只羊,脖子上戴着一条蓝色丝带,还挂着一个铃铛。喜羊羊聪明乐观,总是想出好主意帮助其他伙伴,不让他们被灰太狼吃掉。他的羊朋友包括懒羊羊、美羊羊、沸羊羊和暖羊羊。

作为中国最成功的动画电视连续剧之一,该剧已在中国 75 余家有线电视和卫星电视台播出。它还在包括印度、韩国、马来西亚、新加坡、印度尼西亚、柬埔寨和北美国家在内的 100 多个国家播出。

三、单词点津

1. **series** ['sɪəriːz] *n.* 连续,一系列(事件);(电视、广播等的)系列片

2. **franchise** ['fræntʃaɪz] *n.* 特许经营权;获特许经营权的企业(商店)

3. **ribbon** ['rɪbən] *n.* 丝带,绸带;(表示军功的)绶带,勋带 *v.* 成带状延伸(或运动);把……撕成条带;用缎带装饰

4. **animated** ['ænɪmeɪtɪd] *adj.* 活跃的,生机勃勃的;动画(片)的

四、练习题

选择题

1. According to the article, which statement is true?
   A. Weslie is a goat who wears a blue ribbon with a bell around his waist.

B. Weslie's goat friends include the indolent Paddi, the pretty Tibbi, the hardy Sparky, and the considerate Jonie.

C. The *Pleasant Goat and Big Big Wolf*'s first film is the only super popular one in China.

D. All children and adults love this series but we all have different opinions about it.

2. According to the article, which description is not right about the main character Weslie?

A. He is clever and optimistic.

B. He relies on others to have ideas.

C. He is helpful and warm-hearted.

D. He is happy.

3. Which usage of "ribbon" is wrong?

A. A present was tied with green ribbon.

B. The typewriter needs a new ribbon.

C. We need to ribbon the presents for the New Year.

D. During an opening ceremony, they cut a ribbon.

Do your research and answer these questions orally or by writing.

1. Compared with foreign animated movies, what differences do Chinese animated movies have?

2. Which animated movie is your favorite one and why?

China's village museum trend further advances rural revitalization

(2022.9.22)

The past decade has seen a huge increase in the number of private and public museums being built in China.

According to recent data, by 2021 China had 6,183 **registered** museums throughout the country. They not only cover a diverse **array** of themes and functions, but also have reached a broader range of locations, expanding from urban centers to rural areas to enrich rural **residents' spiritual** lives and promote the **revitalization** of countryside towns and villages.

More rural museums have been **sprouting** like mushrooms after rain in China due to the support of government policies, such as a notice on building digital museums for traditional villages and museums in excellent villages published by the **Ministry of Housing and Urban-Rural Development**.

The basic premise of rural revitalization is to better understand the countryside, and rural museums are seen as significant platforms for furthering this goal. Different places around China, including East China's Zhejiang Province, Northeast China's Jilin Province and North China's Hebei Province, have realized the importance of rural museums and recently approved the establishment of **dozens of** new museums.

一、背景简介

文化不仅是一个国家、一个民族的灵魂，也是一个国家、地区经济社会发展的"软实力"。

过去一提到博物馆，人们第一反应是那是一个"高大上"的地方，只有具有一定规模的城市里才有。令人没有想到的是，进入新世纪以来，特别是随着全面建成小康社会以及乡村振兴战略的深入推进，一座座带着泥土气息的乡村博物馆如雨后春笋般应运而生。尽管各地乡村博物馆内容形式多种多样，但都饱含着当地的文化基因、历史记忆等。可以说，乡村博物馆不仅打通了群众享受公共文化服务"最后一公里"，成为广袤乡间一道多姿多彩的人文风景，也让广大村民拥有了"15 分钟品质文化生活圈"，从而得到更多更好的精神滋养，有助于为农村美好生活"加码"。

二、全文翻译

中国乡村博物馆更好赋能乡村振兴

在过去十年里，中国的私人和公共博物馆数量大幅增加。

根据最新数据，到 2021 年，全中国共有 6,183 家注册博物馆。这些博物馆不仅涵盖了各种主题和功能，而且延伸到更广泛的地区，从城市中心扩展到农村地区，丰富村民的精神生活，促进乡村振兴。

由于政府政策的扶持，如住房和城乡建设部发布的《关于做好中国传统村落数字博物馆优秀村落建馆工作的通知》，越来越多的乡村博物馆在中国如雨后春笋般涌现。

乡村振兴的基本前提是更好地了解乡村，而乡村博物馆是推进这一目标的重要平台。全国各地，包括中国东部的浙江省、东北的吉林省和华北的河北省，都看到了乡村博物馆的重要性，最近批准建立几十座新的博物馆。

三、单词点津

1. **registered** ['redʒɪstəd] *adj.* 已登记的，已注册的。registered capital 注册资金

2. **array** [ə'reɪ] *n.* 一系列，大量 *v.* 布置，排列；配置（兵力）

3. **resident** ['rezɪdənt] *n.* 居民，住户 *adj.* （在某地）居住的，居留的；常驻的

4. **spiritual** ['spɪrɪtʃuəl] *adj.* 精神的，心灵的；宗教的

5. **revitalization** [ˌriːvaɪtəlaɪˈzeɪʃn] *n.* 复兴，复苏

6. **sprout** [spraʊt] *v.* （植物）发芽，生长；涌现 *n.* 苗，新芽，嫩枝

7. **Ministry of Housing and Urban-Rural Development** 住房和城乡建设部

8. **dozens of** 几十；许多

四、难句解析

They not only cover a diverse array of themes and functions, but also have reached a broader range of locations, expanding from urban centers to rural areas to enrich rural residents' spiritual lives and promote the revitalization of countryside towns and villages.

1. **not only…but also…**，意为"不仅……而且……"。

2. **a diverse array of**，意为"各种各样的"；**an array of**，意为"大量的，一批的"。

3. **locations** 后面的 expanding from urban centers to rural areas 为动名词引导的定语从句。

4. **to** 表目的，后面两个并列的目的，一个是 enrich rural residents' spiritual lives（丰富村民精神生活），另一个是 promote the revitalization of countryside towns and villages（促进乡镇和村庄振兴）。

五、练习题

1. According to the article, which statement is true?

   A. The urban center's museums enrich rural residents' spiritual lives.

B. The museums do not cover a diverse array of themes and functions.

C. Only public museums can be registered in China, not the private ones.

D. Many provinces have recently approved the establishment of dozens of new museums.

2. According to the article, what does this mean—"More rural museums have been sprouting like mushrooms after rain in China"?

A. It means every countryside is planting mushrooms.

B. It means more rural museums are displaying mushrooms.

C. With the new policy, the number of the museums is growing quickly.

D. It just means rain helps mushrooms grow.

3. Which word below is not a synonym of "revitalization"?

A. Recovery.

B. Revival.

C. Improvement.

D. Renewal.

Do your research and answer these questions orally or by writing.

1. Do you think museums are important to our lives and why?

2. Are there any museums you visit often and would you please share your experience with us?

New exhibition tackles climate action through art

(2022.9.22)

A total of 15 artists are bringing their understanding and thoughts on the relationship between human beings and nature at an ongoing exhibition at the Inter Art Center & Gallery. The China Climate Action Week **Thematic** Exhibition hosted by the **World Wide Fund for Nature (WWF)** is hosting artists like Carla Chan, Mark Dorf and Qiu Yu, who are presenting their creative works for art and nature lovers in Beijing.

As an independent **curator** focusing on climate change and ecological crises, Wang Naiyi said he hopes these artists from all over the world can rethink their **interdependence** with nature in a **multi-faceted** way, examine the urgent climate crisis and discuss art, while also practicing how to effectively engage and promote climate action.

Creating fun through **interaction**, When Breath Speaks by Su Yongjian and Ba Ruiyun easily captures visitors' attention. The bodies of participants are connected by a white cloth, fitted around the neck so that participants can only see each other's heads. Atop this white plane are bubble helmets floating in space. When **carbon dioxide** sensors detect people's breaths in the bubbles, the **tentacle** devices will swing. As these tentacles draw near each other, they produce a bird-like twittering sound.

一、背景简介

为纪念中国"双碳"目标的提出，世界自然基金会（瑞士）北京代表处与生态环境部宣传教育中心正式联合发起"气候行动周"系列活动，以提升公众对碳中和的意识和理解，获得参与实现碳中和的动力。

气候行动周艺术公益展由世界自然基金会（瑞士）北京代表处主办，邀请了来自全球的 15 位先锋艺术家，以多元的方式重新思考自身与自然的依存关系，共同审视当下迫切的气候危机，探讨艺术实践如何有效地参与并促进气候行动。当全球目光聚焦气候变迁之时，艺术并未置身事外。艺术可以成为改变人们对气候变化的感知、理解和行为的有力工具。

二、全文翻译

新展览通过艺术参与气候行动

　　在映艺术中心·映画廊举办的一场展览上，15 位艺术家展示了他们对人与自然关系的理解和思考。由世界自然基金会（WWF）在北京主办的气候行动周艺术公益展将邀请卡娜、马克·多尔夫和邱宇等艺术家为艺术爱好者和自然保护者们展示其创意作品。

　　关注气候变化和生态危机的独立策展人王乃一表示，他希望来自世界各地的艺术家能够以多元化方式重新思考自身与自然的相互依存关系，审视紧迫的气候变化挑战，讨论艺术的同时探讨如何有效地参与和促进气候行动。

　　苏永建和巴瑞云的《当呼吸可以言语》通过互动创造乐趣，吸引了游客的注意。参与者的身体被白布相连，白布以上，他们只看得到彼此的脑袋。白布上是悬浮的气泡头盔。当二氧化碳传感器检测到人们在气泡中的呼吸时，"触角"装置就会四处摇摆。当两对触角相互靠拢时，它们会发出类似鸟鸣的啸叫声。

三、单词点津

1. **thematic** [θɪˈmætɪk] *adj.* 主题的；专题的
2. **World Wide Fund for Nature (WWF)** 世界自然基金会是在全球享有盛誉的、最大的独立性非政府环境保护组织之一，自 1961 年成立以来，WWF 一直致力于环保事业，在全世界拥有超过 500 万支持者和超过 100 个国家参与的项目网络。
3. **curator** [kjʊəˈreɪtə(r)] *n.* （博物馆）馆长；策展人
4. **interdependence** [ˌɪntədɪˈpendəns] *n.* 互相依赖。其构成为 inter + dependence。

5. **multi-faceted** [ˌmʌltɪˈfæsɪtɪd] *adj.* 多方面的；多才多艺的
6. **interaction** [ˌɪntərˈækʃən] *n.* 互动，交流；相互影响，相互作用
7. **carbon dioxide** 二氧化碳
8. **tentacle** [ˈtentəkl] *n.* [动] 触手，触须

四、难句解析

When carbon dioxide sensors detect people's breaths in the bubbles, the tentacle devices will swing.

when 引导时间状语从句，表示"当……的时候"，when 既可以指时间段，也可指时间点，从句中既可用延续性动词，也可用非延续性动词，且动作既可和主句的动作同时发生，又可在主句的动作之前或之后发生。

五、练习题

1. According to the article, which statement is correct?
   A. Wang Naiyi said he hopes these artists from all over China can reconsider their dependence with nature in a multi-faceted way.
   B. When Breath Speaks by Su Yongjian and Ba Ruiyun interacts with people.
   C. When Breath Speaks by Su Yongjian and Ba Ruiyun hardly captures visitors' attention.
   D. When the carbon dioxide sensors feel people's breaths in the bubbles, the tentacle devices will grow.

2. According to the article, what does this mean—"these artists from all over the world can rethink their interdependence with nature in a multi-faceted way"?

A. These artists should understand that they are not independent from nature.

B. These artists should each represent one country.

C. These artists are all considering this matter from the same angle.

D. These artists should think many times.

3 Which description is correct for "tentacle"?

A. Equipment which can touch people.

B. Hands and arms.

C. The long thin parts that are used for feeling and holding things.

D. Decoration.

Do your research and answer these questions orally or by writing.

1 Are you an art and nature lover? What do you think about the relationship between art and nature?

2 If you were an exhibition curator, how would you like to demonstrate climate change and ecological crises?

Chinese musicians seek to broaden traditional music's influence through creativity and international cooperation

(2022.9.13)

As three performers dressed in traditional Chinese opera costumes perform a scene from Liyuan Opera, an 800-year-old branch of Chinese Opera, the sound of modern pop music **instruments** such as the guitar, drums and **synthesizer** suddenly merge with the ancient music, turning the familiar performance into something that feels fresh and new.

This performance was part of a concert held in Quanzhou, East China's Fujian Province, over the Mid-Autumn Festival weekend to show the charm of Liyuan Opera, one of China's many national **intangible** cultural heritages.

Combining modern pop musical elements and centuries-old traditional music, the performers have **injected** this ancient art form with new vitality as they seek to answer the question: How can traditional Chinese music gain the attention of younger audiences in China and the rest of the world?

一、背景简介

梨园戏是中国福建省的汉族戏曲之一，也是闽南语系的传统地方戏剧之一。梨园戏发源于宋元时期的泉州，与浙江的南戏并称为"搬演南宋戏文唱念声腔"的"闽浙之音"，被誉为"古南戏活化石"。

二、全文翻译

中国音乐家们通过创意和国际合作扩大传统音乐的影响力

当三名身着中国传统戏曲服装的演员表演已有八百年历史的中国戏

曲分支梨园戏的一幕时，吉他、鼓和合成器等现代流行音乐乐器的声音蓦然融合进了古典音乐，将大众熟悉的表演变得充满新鲜感。

这场演出是中国东部福建省泉州市于中秋节周末举行的音乐会的一个环节，旨在展示中国非物质文化遗产之一梨园戏的魅力。

表演者将现代流行音乐元素与有着数百年历史的传统音乐相结合，为这一古老的艺术形式注入了新的活力，他们试图回答这样一个问题：中国传统音乐如何吸引中国和世界其他地区的年轻观众？

三、单词点津

1. **instrument** ['ɪnstrəmənt] *n.* 器械；乐器；仪器；促成某事的人（或事物）；手段
2. **synthesizer** ['sɪnθəsaɪzə(r)] *n.* [电子] 合成器
3. **intangible** [ɪn'tændʒəbl] *adj.* 不可捉摸的；难以确定的；（资产、利益）无形的 *n.* 无形的东西
4. **inject** [ɪn'dʒekt] *v.* 注射；（给……）添加；投入（金钱或资源）

四、难句解析

Combining modern pop musical elements and centuries-old traditional music, the performers have injected this ancient art form with new vitality as they seek to answer the question.

1. **combining**，现在分词作非谓语动词，主语是 the performers。
2. **have injected**，是现在完成时。
3. **as** 表示"当、随着"，引导时间状语从句。

五、练习题

1. According to the article, which statement is correct?

   A. The combination of traditional and modern music turned

the familiar performance into something that feels fresh and new.

B. The combining of modern pop musical elements and centuries-old traditional music is not possible.

C. The artists have successfully answered the question: How can traditional Chinese music gain the attention of younger audiences in China and the rest of the world?

D. The Liyuan Opera used to be one of China's many national intangible cultural heritages.

2 According to the article, how do we understand "the performers have injected this ancient art form with new vitality"?

A. The performers put these two things into the same container.

B. The performers use a needle to put vitality into ancient art.

C. The performers put some new medicine into the ancient art.

D. The performers combine the traditional music with the sound of the guitar, drums and synthesizer.

3 Which explanation is not right for "intangible"?

A. Cannot be touched.

B. Incapable of being perceived by the senses.

C. Lacking substance or reality.

D. Easy to recognize.

问答题

Do your research and answer these questions orally or by writing.

1 Do you know about any other Chinese national intangible cultural heritages? If so, what are they?

2 How can traditional Chinese music gain the attention of younger audiences in China and the rest of the world?

第9篇

New exhibition in Beijing highlights Hong Kong urban design and development over past 25 years

(2022.9.21)

As part of the celebration of the 25th anniversary of Hong Kong's return to the motherland, the *Beyond Territories—Made, Make, Making* exhibition hosted by the Hong Kong Institute of Architects aims to give mainlanders more opportunities to learn more about Hongkongers and how they created a city with a unique **dense** and diverse aesthetics.

The "significant exhibition, telling the great story of Hong Kong architects" will have mainlanders "celebrate the 25th anniversary of the establishment of the Hong Kong Special Administrative Region together" through a series of inspiring **architectural** designs exploring the **populated** and diverse Hong Kong and **savoring** the city's **tenacious** spirit and unique landscape, said Hong Kong Chief Executive John Lee Ka-chiu in a pre-recorded video during the opening.

According to the exhibition's curators, considering the city's diverse culture and rich traditions, Hong Kong architects have always aspired to create a **sustainable** city and **strived to** bridge the gap between the past and future by using their expertise and paying close attention to heritage conservation practices while also taking into account technological innovation.

一、背景简介

2022 年 9 月 20 日，由香港建筑师学会主办的城市规划建筑设计成就展《越界——回忆·实现·变进》系列巡回展北京站开幕。来自京港两地的建筑业界、专业院校、跨界文化和设计领域的工作者、专家和学者出席，共同庆祝香港回归祖国 25 周年。这次展览共有超过 40 组香港及海外单位参展，设有"回忆""实现""变进"3个主题展区，呈现香港的发展历程，展示一系列富有启发性的建筑项目和设计作品，让观众前来探索多元香港，细味其坚韧的人文精神与独特的地方风貌。

二、全文翻译

北京新展呈现香港过去25年的城市设计和发展

作为庆祝香港回归25周年活动的一部分，香港建筑师学会主办的"越界——回忆·实现·变进"展览旨在让内地有更多机会了解香港，品味其缜密、多元的独特城市美学。

香港特别行政区行政长官李家超在开幕式致辞视频中说，"香港城市规划建筑设计成就展"将通过一系列富有启发性的建筑设计，让内地观众"共同庆祝香港特别行政区成立25周年"，探索人口众多、风格多样的香港，品味其坚忍的人文精神和独特的地方风貌。

据此次展览的策展人介绍，考虑到香港多元的文化和丰富的传统，香港建筑师一直致力于创建一个可持续发展的城市，利用他们的专业知识努力弥合过去和未来的差距，密切关注文物保护措施的同时也关注技术创新。

三、单词点津

1. **dense** [dens] *adj.* 稠密的；浓密的；浓重的；密度大的
2. **architectural** [ɑ:kɪˈtektʃərəl] *adj.* 建筑学的；建筑方面的
3. **populated** [ˈpɒpjuleɪtɪd] *adj.* 有人口居住的
4. **savor** [ˈseɪvə(r)] *v.* 尽情享受；品尝
5. **tenacious** [təˈneɪʃəs] *adj.* 顽强的；坚持的
6. **sustainable** [səˈsteɪnəbl] *adj.* （计划、方法、体制）持续性的；（自然资源）可持续的
7. **strive to do** 努力做……

四、练习题

1. According to the article, which statement is true?

   A. Hong Kong architects have always aspired to create a sustainable city and differentiate the past and future.

   B. The presentation by Hong Kong Chief Executive John Lee Ka-chiu was through live video during the opening.

   C. Hong Kong architects have always attached great importance to heritage conservation practices while also taking into account technological innovation.

   D. The *Beyond Territories—Made, Make, Making* exhibition hosted by the Hong Kong Institute of Architects aims to inform Hong Kong people to understand how mainland people think.

2. According to the article, how do you understand "The significant exhibition, telling the great story of Hong Kong architects"?

   A. Stories showing the gap between the past and future.

   B. Stories showing a series of inspiring architectural designs.

   C. Stories showing how populated and diverse Hong Kong is.

   D. Stories showing Hong Kong's tenacious spirit.

3. Which word below is not a synonym of "tenacious"?

   A. Tough.

   B. Optimistic.

   C. Steadfast.

   D. Persistent.

Do your research and answer these questions orally or by writing.

1. What do you think about your hometown's spirit and culture? How is it different from other places in China?

2. If you were asked to present a city's spirit and culture, in which way would you like to do the exhibition?

Chinese vloggers promote traditional culture around the world by innovating on inheritance

(2022.9.21)

Hundreds of young content creators who are fond of traditional culture and Chinese fashion are set to gather together in East China's Jiangsu Province during the upcoming National Day holidays for a grand cultural event, where they will wear **exquisite** traditional clothing and enjoy performances of ancient art forms such as Chinese opera.

At Guofeng Dadian 2022 (Grand ceremony of Chinese style), these young creatives will bring participants back to ancient **dynasties** so visitors can experience the life of their ancestors through activities such as **strolling through** fairs and enjoying tea with friends.

They will also take to the catwalk to display traditional clothing, play Chinese musical instruments at concerts and show off the intangible cultural heritage skills they have inherited from past generations.

These content creators are the **epitome** of the huge number of young people in China who are addicted to tradition and **eagerly** produce works such as videos about ancient China's charm to share their enthusiasm with domestic and overseas audiences.

一、背景简介

近年来，国风文化焕发新生，国风之美也在大批年轻人中备受推崇，并逐渐成为一种流行的生活方式。作为国风江湖的超级 IP，"国风大典"对传统文化秉承创新性传承的态度，选择契合年轻群体需求，用国风与 Z

世代沟通。除了在审美层面上运用年轻潮流之势多元展现国风之美外，"国风大典"还深入价值与情感层面，以国风文化带来积极情感体验，激发民族自豪感，实现更深层次的价值认同。2022年已是"国风大典"的第三届，其凭借在形式、内容等多方面的创新和巨量引擎传播矩阵与流量势能的加持，不断地衍生出全新的多样态内容与价值。一个国风领域的头部内容IP，正在释放出它的巨大能量。"国风大典"除了营造更为浓厚的国风文化氛围外，也极大丰富了视听形式，拓宽了国风的表达边界，助推国风文化不断实现破圈传播。而其所构建起的内容"引力场"，也为众多品牌找到了"同路人"，共同为优秀传统文化注入新能量。

二、全文翻译

视频博主通过传承创新在世界传播中国传统文化

数百名热爱传统文化和中国时尚的年轻博主将在国庆假期齐聚中国东部的江苏省，参加一场文化盛典，他们将穿着美轮美奂的汉服，欣赏京剧等传统艺术表演。

在2022年国风大典上，这些年轻的创意者将带游客穿越回古代，游客可以通过各种活动体验古人的生活，比如逛集市，与友人饮茶等。

他们还将在T台上进行汉服展示，在音乐会上演奏中国乐器，并展示他们从先辈手中传承下来的非物质文化遗产。

这些博主是中国当代众多年轻人的缩影，他们热爱传统文化，制作视频作品以展现中国传统文化魅力，并与国内外观众分享对国风的热爱。

三、单词点津

1. **exquisite** [ɪkˈskwɪzɪt] *adj.* 精致的，精美的
2. **dynasty** [ˈdɪnəsti] *n.* 王朝；朝，代
3. **stroll through** 漫步在
4. **epitome** [ɪˈpɪtəmi] *n.* 典型，缩影；摘要，概要
5. **eagerly** [ˈiːɡəlɪ] *adv.* 急切地；渴望地；热心地

四、难句解析

Hundreds of young content creators who are fond of traditional culture and Chinese fashion are set to gather together in East China's Jiangsu Province during the upcoming National Day holidays for a grand cultural event, where they will wear exquisite traditional clothing and enjoy performances of ancient art forms such as Chinese opera.

1. 句子中包含两个定语从句，一个是 who 引导的定语从句，修饰前面的 creators；一个是 where 引导的定语从句，修饰前面的 event。

2. 关于介词的使用，省份之前用 in，"在……期间"用 during，表目的用 for。

五、练习题

1. According to the article, which statement is true?

   A. These content creators want to produce videos about ancient China's charm exclusively to the Chinese audience.

   B. They play Chinese musical instruments with western instruments at concerts.

   C. The young creative artists will meet in Western China.

   D. During the Guofeng Dadian 2022, people can experience ancient dynasties.

2. During the Guofeng Dadian 2022, which activity isn't mentioned in the article?

   A. Watch Chinese opera.

   B. Walk around in the fairs.

C. Teach foreigners Chinese.

D. Wear traditional clothing.

3 Which word below is not a synonym of "stroll"?

A. Walk.

B. Explore.

C. Wander.

D. Roam.

Do your research and answer these questions orally or by writing.

1 If you were asked to promote Chinese culture around the world, how would you do it?

2 Among the Chinese promotional bloggers, who do you like the most and why?

3 Although people enjoy today's modern life, why do some miss the traditional lifestyle?

'Qinqiang' inspired song cheers in e-sport game

(2022.9.22)

For the first time, **top-tier** e-sport video game *Counter-Strike: Global Offensive* (CS:GO) has included a Chinese song in the game.

Instead of a pop hit or a **contemporary** classic, the developers turned to music from the traditional intangible cultural heritage known as Qinqiang Opera for inspiration.

Released on Wednesday, the battle song "Hualian (Painted face)," which combines the melody of Qinqiang Opera with rock'n'roll, will **commemorate** the 5th anniversary of the game's launch in China. This is the first song to include traditional Chinese **elements** that the game has added to its music library since CS:GO was first introduced to the world in 2012.

The game is operated in China solely by Perfect World esprots, and the **release** of "Hualian" means that players around the world can experience the **sensational** feeling brought by Qinqiang Opera, a treasure of traditional Chinese culture, while playing the game.

一、背景简介

秦腔是起源于古代陕西、甘肃一带的汉族民间戏剧,在中国古代政治经济、文化中心长安生长壮大,经历代人民的创造而逐渐形成,因周代以来,关中地区就被称为"秦",秦腔由此而得名。因以枣木梆子为击节乐器,又叫"梆子腔"。作为中国汉族最古老的戏曲剧种之一,一直深受西北地区人民的喜爱。如今,中国非遗文化中的艺术瑰宝——秦腔与电竞展开联动,让全世界听到来自中国西北大地的旋律。

二、全文翻译

"秦腔"主题曲唱响电子竞技游戏

顶级电子竞技游戏《反恐精英:全球攻势》(CS: GO)首次在游戏中收录了一首中文歌曲。

开发人员没有选择流行歌曲或当代经典歌曲,而是从传统非物质文化遗产秦腔中寻找灵感。

周三发布的主题战歌《花脸》将秦腔的旋律与摇滚乐相结合,纪念该游戏在中国上线5周年。这是自2012年CS: GO首次发行以来,首次收录的包含中国传统元素的中文音乐盒。

游戏由完美世界电竞公司在中国独家运营,《花脸》的发行意味着全球玩家可以在游戏中享受中国传统文化瑰宝秦腔带来的听觉盛宴。

三、单词点津

1. **top-tier** [tɒp tɪə(r)] *adj.* 顶尖的

2. **contemporary** [kən'temprəri] *adj.* 当代的;现代的;同时代的 *n.* 同时代的人;同龄人,同辈。contemporary literature 现代文学

3. **commemorate** [kə'meməreɪt] *v.* 纪念,用以纪念

4. **element** ['elɪmənt] *n.* 要素;元素

5. **release** [rɪ'liːs] *v.* 释放,放走;解救;松开;公布,发行 *n.* 释放;泄漏;宣泄;解脱;公映

6. **sensational** [sen'seɪʃnl] *adj.* 轰动的,激动人心的;夸张的

四、难句解析

This is the first song to include traditional Chinese elements that the game has added to its music library since CS:GO was first introduced to the world in 2012.

1. the first (thing) to do sth.,意为"第一个做某事"。

2 **that** 引导定语从句，修饰前面的 elements。

3 句子中有 since，前面用完成时。

五、练习题

1 What was the genre of the song that was put into CS:GO?

    A. Chinese Rock and roll.

    B. Chinese pop music.

    C. Traditional Chinese opera.

    D. Chinese Folk music.

2 Who is in charge of operating the game in China?

    A. Chinese gaming.

    B. Wechat.

    C. Valve.

    D. Perfect World.

3 Which word is not a synonym of "sensational"?

    A. Amazing.

    B. Ordinary.

    C. Astonishing.

    D. Thrilling.

Do your research and answer these questions orally or by writing.

1 How do you create a balance between gaming and real life?

2 What are the positives and negatives of playing games?

扫一扫，听音频

第四部分 政经
Politics and Economy

China-built expressway in Nairobi, Kenya, starts trial operation

(2022.5.15)

An **expressway** built by a Chinese enterprise in **Nairobi**, Kenya's capital, started **trial** operation on Saturday, the Xinhua News Agency reported, showcasing closer cooperation between China and Kenya under the **Belt and Road Initiative (BRI)**.

The expressway, constructed by the China Road and Bridge Corporation (CRBC), connects the country's important **landmarks** from downtown Nairobi to an international airport, covering a total length of 27.1 kilometers.

The road, a **flagship** project under the China-proposed BRI, marks the enhanced cooperation between China and Kenya and the broader African **continent**, experts noted.

The project is the first toll road in the country, developed by the CRBC in partnership with the Kenyan government, with a total construction and operation period of 30 years. After 30 years, the entire expressway, equipment, and technology will be **handed over** to the Kenyan government free of charge.

一、背景简介

2022年5月14日,由中国路桥工程有限责任公司投资开发和建设运营的肯尼亚首都内罗毕快速路启动试运营。内罗毕快速路连接内罗毕市区与乔莫·肯雅塔国际机场,途经内罗毕中央商务区、国家博物馆、国家体育场、议会大厦、总统府等重要地标,全长27.1公里,于2020年9月启动施工建设。内罗毕快速路运营后,可显著缓解市区拥堵,缩短市区往返乔莫·肯雅塔国际机场的通勤时间,提升内罗毕城市形象,为当地创造大量就业机会,推动经济社会发展,造福当地人民。

二、全文翻译

中国在肯尼亚内罗毕修建的快速路开始试运行

据新华社报道,一家中国企业在肯尼亚首都内罗毕修建的快速路于周六开始试运营,这表明中国和肯尼亚在"一带一路"倡议(BRI)下的合作更加密切。

这条快速路由中国路桥工程有限责任公司(CRBC)建造,连接内罗毕市中心到国际机场之间的重要地标建筑,全长27.1公里。

专家指出,这条快速路是中国提出的"一带一路"倡议下的旗舰项目,标志着中国与肯尼亚以及非洲其他地区合作的加强。

该项目是该国第一条收费公路,由中国路桥与肯尼亚政府合作开发,总建设和经营期为30年。30年后,整条快速路及相关设备、技术将免费移交给肯尼亚政府。

三、单词点津

1. **expressway** [ɪkˈspresweɪ] *n.* 高速公路,快速路
2. **Nairobi** [ˌnaɪəˈrəubi] *n.* 内罗毕(肯尼亚首都)
3. **trial** [ˈtraɪəl] *n.* 审判;试用;(对人的忍耐、自制力的)考验
4. **Belt and Road Initiative (BRI)** "一带一路"是"丝绸之路经济带"和"21世纪海上丝绸之路"的简称。2013年9月和10

月由中国国家主席习近平分别提出建设"新丝绸之路经济带"和"21世纪海上丝绸之路"的合作倡议。依靠中国与有关国家既有的双多边机制，借助既有的、行之有效的区域合作平台，"一带一路"旨在借用古代丝绸之路的历史符号，高举和平发展的旗帜，积极发展与沿线国家的经济合作伙伴关系，共同打造政治互信、经济融合、文化包容的利益共同体、命运共同体和责任共同体。

5 **landmark** ['lændmɑːk] *n.* 陆标，地标；里程碑

6 **flagship** ['flæɡʃɪp] *n.* 旗舰；同类中佼佼者

7 **continent** ['kɒntɪnənt] *n.* 洲，大陆

8 **hand over** 移交

四、练习题

1 According to the article, which statement is correct?

  A. An expressway built by a Chinese company in Nairobi, started official operation on Saturday.

  B. The expressway constructed by the China Road and Bridge Corporation, will connect China and Nairobi, Kenya's capital.

  C. The project is the first toll road in the country, with a total construction and operation period of 30 years.

  D. This flagship project will establish roads that connect not only China and Kenya but also China and the broader African continent.

2 How long is the expressway constructed by the China Road and Bridge Corporation (CRBC)?

  A. From the airport to downtown.

  B. 25 kilometers.

C. 27.1 kilometers.

D. Within Kenya's capital.

3 Which is not a synonym of "landmark"?

A. Beacon.

B. International.

C. Indicator.

D. Signal.

Do your research and answer these questions orally or by writing.

1 Why did we cooperate with the Kenyan government and establish the expressway in Kenya?

2 What do you think as a country we should do to enhance our cooperation with other countries?

'Polar Silk Road' eyes new vision amid global challenges

(2021.10.21)

The Polar Silk Road has recently gained **renewed** attention following its rapid growth in supporting regional economy and securing energy supplies amid **volatility** throughout global supply chains posed by an ongoing **pandemic** in many parts of the world.

During the recent 2021 Arctic Circle Assembly hosted in Iceland, the Polar Silk Road, proposed by leaders of China and Russia in 2017, came under the spotlight as the melting of **Arctic** sea ice has made it possible for **merchant** ships to **navigate** the Arctic Ocean, greatly shortening shipping lanes connecting Asia and Europe and even North America.

Participants at the **assembly** said opening the Arctic route will promote the overall growth of the economy in the region and the global trade and shipping pattern will **undergo** major changes. Experts said that the Polar Silk Road will be an important direction for exploration as part of the Belt and Road Initiative (BRI).

一、背景简介

如今,无论从经济上还是从军事安全上来说,北极都是世界上主要的地区之一。冰川的融化不仅打开了以前人迹罕至的地区,而且也打开了北半球与北欧主要国家。随着极地冰以创纪录的速度减少,北极的发展开辟了新的贸易路线。北极在中国的外交和经济政策中发挥着越来越重要的作用。2018年1月,中国政府发布了北极战略,并将其视为"一带一路"倡议的一部分。北极地区可能成为原材料来源地和连接东亚与欧洲的运输路线。

二、全文翻译

"极地丝绸之路"在全球挑战中展现新愿景

最近,极地丝绸之路再次受到关注。在世界许多地区的持续疫情造成全球供应链波动的情况下,极地丝绸之路在支持区域经济和保障能源供给方面取得迅速发展。

在最近于冰岛举行的 2021 年北极圈论坛上,中俄领导人于 2017 年提出的极地丝绸之路成为人们关注的焦点,因为北冰洋冰川的融化使商船能够航行,大大缩短了连接亚洲、欧洲甚至北美的航线。

与会者表示,开通北极航线将促进该地区经济的整体增长,全球贸易和航运格局将发生重大变化。专家表示,极地丝绸之路将是"一带一路"倡议的一个重要探索方向。

三、单词点津

1. **renewed** [rɪ'nju:d] *adj.* 再次发生的;再次兴起的;重新振作的
2. **volatility** [ˌvɒlə'tɪlɪti] *n.* 易变;活泼;挥发性
3. **pandemic** [pæn'demɪk] *n.* 大流行病
4. **Arctic** ['ɑ:ktɪk] *adj.* 北极的　*n.* 北极,北极地区
5. **merchant** ['mɜ:tʃənt] *n.* 商人　*adj.* 海上货运的
6. **navigate** ['nævɪgeɪt] *v.* 导航;航行于
7. **assembly** [ə'sembli] *n.* 议会,代表大会;集会;集会者
8. **undergo** [ˌʌndə'gəʊ] *v.* 经历,经受

四、难句解析

…the Polar Silk Road, proposed by leaders of China and Russia in 2017, came under the spotlight as the melting of Arctic sea ice has made it possible for merchant ships to navigate the Arctic Ocean, greatly shortening shipping lanes connecting Asia and Europe and even North America.

1. **proposed by leaders of China and Russia in 2017** 为非限制性定语从句,省略了引导词 **which** 和 **be** 动词。

② **as the melting…，as**为连词，引导原因状语从句。

五、练习题

① According to the article, which statement is true?

A. For the first time, the Polar Silk Road has recently gained attention following its rapid growth in supporting the regional economy.

B. The recent 2021 Arctic Circle Assembly hosted in Iceland, was proposed by leaders of China and Russia in 2017.

C. The melting of Arctic sea ice has provided a short cut for merchant ships heading through the Arctic Ocean, connecting Asia, Europe, and even North America.

D. Participants at the assembly said global trade and shipping patterns have already had major changes.

② What make it possible for merchant ships to navigate the Arctic Ocean?

A. The volatility throughout global supply chains.

B. Participants at the assembly.

C. 2021 Arctic Circle Assembly.

D. The melting of Arctic sea ice.

③ Which is not a synonym of "undergo"?

A. Repair.

B. Experience.

C. Encounter.

D. Endure.

Do your research and answer these questions orally or by writing.

① What is the meaning of the Polar Silk Road?

② With the melting of the Arctic sea ice, what other things will happen?

China's national carbon market celebrates one year anniversary, becoming world's largest

(2022.7.17)

It has been a year since China's national carbon market started online trading in Shanghai on July 16, 2021. As of Friday, the **cumulative** trading **volume** of the carbon market reached 194 million tons, with a cumulative **turnover** of 8.49 billion yuan ($1.26 billion), according to data released by the Shanghai Environment and Energy Exchange (SEEE).

One year on, the smooth operation of the carbon market reflects the **significant** progress made by the country to promote reduction of carbon **emission**. It has helped to form the function of carbon pricing, Ma Jun, director of the Beijing-based Institute of Public and Environmental Affairs, told the *Global Times* on Saturday.

Carbon trading is the process of buying and selling permits to **emit** carbon dioxide or other greenhouse gases. Ma said that this type of high-**efficiency market-oriented** approach is needed to reach peak carbon dioxide emissions by 2030 and achieve carbon **neutrality** by 2060.

一、背景简介

2020年9月，中国向世界做出实现"双碳"目标的承诺，中国进入"双碳"时代。以2021年7月16日为标志，全国碳排放交易市场进入了运行、发展、完善的新阶段，截至目前，全国碳市场成功运行一周年。建设全国碳市场是我国应对气候变化的一项重大制度创新，据生态环境部有关负责人介绍，碳市场运行一年来，在确保电力供应的前提下，对高效机组进行激励，对低效机组进行约束，成为推动电力行业低碳绿色转型的"指挥棒"，促进了企业探索节能减排绿色发展的新路。上海环境能源交易所数据显示，截至 2022 年 7 月 13 日收盘，全国碳市场累计成交量约 1.94 亿吨，累计成交额约 84.9 亿元，已经成为全球覆盖温室气体排放量规模最大的碳市场。

二、全文翻译

中国全国碳市场一周年，成为全球最大碳市场

2021 年 7 月 16 日，中国全国碳市场在上海开始线上交易，至此已有一年。上海环境能源交易所（SEEE）发布数据显示，截至周五，全国碳市场的累计成交量达到 1.94 亿吨，累计成交额 84.9 亿元人民币（12.6 亿美元）。

过去一年，碳市场的平稳运行反映了中国在促进碳减排方面取得的重大进展。北京公众环境研究中心主任马军周六接受《环球时报》采访时表示，这有助于形成碳定价的功能。

碳交易是买卖二氧化碳或其他温室气体排放配额的过程。马军表示，要在 2030 年前达到二氧化碳排放峰值，并在 2060 年前实现碳中和，需要这种高效的市场导向方式。

三、单词点津

1. **cumulative** [ˈkjuːmjələtɪv] *adj.* 积累的，渐增的；累计的
2. **volume** [ˈvɒljuːm] *n.* 体积；容积
3. **turnover** [ˈtɜːnəʊvə(r)] *n.* （一定时期内的）营业额，成交量
4. **significant** [sɪɡˈnɪfɪkənt] *adj.* 显著的；相当数量的；重要的。名词形式为 significance，意为"重要性，意义"。
5. **emission** [ɪˈmɪʃn] *n.* 排放物，散发物；（尤指光、热、气等的）散发，排放。动词形式是 emit，意为"排放，散发"。
6. **efficiency** [ɪˈfɪʃnsi] *n.* 效率，效能
7. **market-oriented** *adj.* 市场导向的
8. **neutrality** [njuːˈtræləti] *n.* 中立，中立状态

四、练习题

1. According to the article, which of the following statements is correct?

   A. Carbon trading is the platform for buying and selling carbon.

   B. On July 16th, 2021, the current trading volume of the carbon market was 194 million tons.

   C. The reductions of carbon emissions can be measured by the carbon market.

   D. At the one year anniversary, China's national carbon market is going to become the world's largest market.

2. According to the article, why does the smooth operation of the carbon market reflect the important progress made by the country to promote reduction of carbon emission?

   A. Due to the UN goal of peak carbon emissions in 2030.

   B. Because of China's goal to reach peak carbon emissions by 2030.

   C. The public have decided to start reducing carbon emissions.

   D. Foreign experts proposed the idea to reduce carbon emissions.

3. Which word below is not a synonym of "cumulative"?

   A. Accumulative.

   B. Expectation.

   C. Increasing.

   D. Adding.

Do your research and answer these questions orally or by writing.

1. What do you know about China's national carbon market?

2. How important is it for our country to achieve carbon neutrality and why?

Dunhuang Research Institute, Tencent to launch digital scripture cave of Mogao Grottoes

(2022.6.15)

The Dunhuang Research Institute and Tencent on Wednesday launched a digital **laboratory** to build a **full-scale** digital **scripture** cave online of the world-famous Mogao **Grottoes**, sharing with the public the "fresh life" behind the cultural relics in an interactive experience.

They will use laser **scanning** and photo **reconstruction** technology, combined with **procedural** content generation and physically based rendering technologies, to **restore** the details of the ancient paintings and cultural relics with millimeter-level **accuracy** 1:1, and simulate the lighting and **vegetation** of the Mogao Grottoes in Dunhuang at different times, in a bid to build a full-scale digital scripture cave online, according to a release Tencent sent to the *Global Times*.

The two parties signed a five-year strategic cooperation agreement. Based on the technology laboratory and using the game technology of Tencent Interactive Entertainment, they will jointly develop cultural and creative **intellectual property** (IP) products and carry out in-depth cooperation in many fields.

一、背景简介

敦煌藏经洞是中国 20 世纪最伟大的考古发现之一。洞窟内藏有公元 4 世纪到公元 11 世纪的经卷、文书、绢画等 6 万余件文物，被称为"打开世界中世纪历史的钥匙"。然而，因为历史原因，这些珍贵文物流散到世界各地，大部分人无缘窥见其真貌。由敦煌研究院和腾讯联手打造的"腾讯互娱×数字敦煌文化遗产数字创意技术联合实验室"（以下简称"技术实验室")于 2022 年 6 月正式宣布成立。发布会上,技术实验室宣布启动首批合作项目"数字藏经洞和敦煌莫高窟官方虚拟人伽瑶"的相关工作。技术实验室将结合敦煌研究院的文物数字化技术和腾讯互娱的游戏技术在线上构建一个全真的数字藏经洞,以互动体验的方式和大众一同分享藏经洞出土文物背后的"鲜活历史",还将打造出敦煌莫高窟官方虚拟人伽瑶,开展虚拟人实时直播、讲解等具体实践,为弘扬敦煌文化探索创新演绎方式。

二、全文翻译

敦煌研究院、腾讯将推出莫高窟数字藏经洞

敦煌研究院和腾讯于周三启动数字实验室,在线上构建了一个全真的莫高窟数字藏经洞,以互动体验的方式与公众分享文物背后的"生动故事"。

据腾讯提供给《环球时报》的新闻报道称,他们希望在线上构建一个全真的数字藏经洞。他们将使用激光扫描和照片重建技术,结合程序化内容生成技术和基于物理的渲染技术,以毫米级的精度 1∶1 还原壁画和文物的细节,并模拟不同时间敦煌莫高窟里的光照和植被情况。

双方签署了一项为期五年的战略合作协议。技术实验室将利用腾讯互动娱乐的游戏技术,共同开发文化创意知识产权产品,并在多个领域开展深度合作。

三、单词点津

1. **laboratory** [ləˈbɒrətri] *n.* 实验室
2. **full-scale** [ˌfʊl ˈskeɪl] *adj.* 全面的;完全的;照原尺寸的
3. **scripture** [ˈskrɪptʃə(r)] *n.* (某一宗教的)经文,圣典
4. **grotto** [ˈgrɒtəʊ] *n.* (人工)洞穴
5. **scan** [skæn] *vt.* 细看,审视;浏览;扫描检查
6. **reconstruction** [ˌriːkənˈstrʌkʃn] *n.* 再建,重建;改造
7. **procedural** [prəˈsiːdʒərəl] *adj.* 程序上的

8. **restore** [rɪˈstɔː(r)] *v.* 恢复（某种情况或感受）；使复原
9. **accuracy** [ˈækjərəsi] *n.* 准确性，精确性
10. **vegetation** [ˌvedʒəˈteɪʃn] *n.* （总称）植物，植被
11. **intellectual property** 知识产权

四、难句解析

Based on the technology laboratory and using the game technology of Tencent Interactive Entertainment, they will jointly develop cultural and creative intellectual property (IP) products and carry out in-depth cooperation in many fields.

1. **base** 和 **use** 的时态不同，因为和主语的关系不同。一个是被动，用过去分词；一个是主动，用现在分词。
2. **in many fields**，意为"在很多领域"。
3. **carry out cooperation**，意为"开展合作"。

五、练习题

1. According to the article, which of the following statements is true?

   A. The laboratory will restore the details of the ancient paintings and cultural relics without simulation of lighting and vegetation of the Mogao Grottoes.

   B. The two parties signed a five-year cooperation agreement exclusively focused on the full-scale digital scripture, excluding creative intellectual property products.

   C. A millimeter-level digital scripture cave will be created online by using laser scanning and photo reconstruction technology, as well as procedural content generation and physically based rendering technologies.

    D. The two parties' five-year cooperation agreement will carry on development of cultural and creative intellectual property products and in-depth cooperation in many fields.

2 According to the article, what is the reason behind the two parties wanting to do the digital scripture cave of Mogao Grottoes?

    A. This project can help the two parties make a lot of money.
    B. It was decided by the administration of natural history.
    C. To bring fresh life into the ancient relics and share them with the public.
    D. The two parties are working on the Magao Grottoes together in order to decide on future endeavors.

3 Which word below is not a synonym of "restore"?

    A. Fix.
    B. Repair.
    C. Re-examine.
    D. Renovate.

Do your research and answer these questions orally or by writing.

1 Why do you think that intellectual property products are becoming more popular?

2 A part from the reasons mentioned in the article, what do you think are the reasons for the cooperation between the two parties?

Space seed breeding makes breakthrough, yielding nearly 1,000 new species

(2022.4.27)

With the return of the crew of China's spacecraft Shenzhou-13, a total of 12,000 seeds finished their space **breeding** journey, which is expected to enhance food security, as seeds are as important as chips in the **semiconductor** industry.

Seeds of **clover**, oats, rice, **edible** mushrooms and cabbage were carried by the Shenzhou-13 into space and brought back to Earth on April 16, after 183 days in space.

It has been 35 years since China's first space seed breeding effort in 1987, and nearly 1,000 new species have been created, of which 200 have displayed outstanding **performances**, according to media reports.

China's space seed project has bred lots of vegetable and fruit species, including such common items as apples, Li Guoxiang, a researcher at the Rural Development Institute of the Chinese Academy of Social Sciences, told the *Global Times* on Wednesday.

China's space seed breeding has made a great contribution to the country's food security and **environmental** protection.

一、背景简介

太空育种也称航天育种、空间诱变育种，是利用太空的特殊环境诱使植物种子发生基因变异，进而选育植物新品种、创造农业育种材料、丰富基因资源，是一种将辐射、宇航、育种和遗传等学科综合起来的高新技术。简单来说，让种子先"上天"再"入地"，经过筛选、杂交、鉴定等，最终形成新种质资源的过程就是太空育种。与传统育种技术相比，太空育种最大优势在于空间诱变材料的变异率高、育种周期短，可在相对较短时间内创制出高产、早熟、抗病等性状优良的种质资源。我国太空育种始于 1987 年，先后利用各类航天器，搭载植物种子、菌种、试管苗等 4,000 余种，培育的小麦、水稻、玉米、大豆、棉花和番茄、辣椒等园艺作物新品种，经过国审和省审的航天育种新品种超过 200 个，累计种植面积达 1.5 亿亩。

二、全文翻译

太空育种取得突破，产生近 1,000 个新物种

随着中国神舟十三号飞船机组人员的返回，共有 12,000 颗种子完成了太空繁育之旅，预计这将加强粮食安全，因为种子的重要性堪比芯片在半导体产业中的作用。

4 月 16 日，在太空飞行 183 天后，神舟十三号将三叶草、燕麦、大米、食用菌和卷心菜的种子送入太空并带回地球。

据媒体报道，自 1987 年中国首次太空育种，已经过去了 35 年，创造了近 1,000 个新物种，其中 200 个品种培育结果良好。

中国社会科学院农村发展研究所研究员李国祥周三告诉《环球时报》，中国的太空种子项目已经培育了很多蔬菜和水果品种，包括苹果等常见品种。

中国的航天育种为国家粮食安全和环境保护做出了巨大贡献。

三、单词点津

1. **breed** [briːd] *v.* 饲养，培育；引起　*n.* 品种
2. **semiconductor** [ˌsemikənˈdʌktə(r)] *n.* 半导体；半导体装置
3. **clover** [ˈkləʊvə(r)] *n.* 三叶草
4. **edible** [ˈedəbl] *adj.* 可食用的
5. **performance** [pəˈfɔːməns] *n.* 表演，演出；工作情况；表现
6. **environmental** [ɪnˌvaɪrənˈmentl] *adj.* 自然环境的，生态环境的；环保的

四、难句解析

It has been 35 years since China's first space seed breeding effort in 1987, and nearly 1,000 new species have been created, of which 200 have displayed outstanding performances, according to media reports.

① 句子中出现 **since**，用完成时态。

② **have been created**，现在完成时的被动语态，这里指"物种被创造"。

③ **of which**，which 是关系代词，先行词为 species，200 of the 1,000 species 中的 of 放在关系代词前，of which 引导非限定性定语从句。

五、练习题

1. According to the article, which of the following statements is correct?

   A. The seeds which finished their space breeding journey include clover, rice, all mushrooms, cabbage and oats.

   B. Among the nearly 1,000 new species created during the space seed breeding, 200 of them showed prominent abilities.

   C. The space seed breeding journey started in 1987 and more than 1,000 species have been created.

   D. China's space seed project only breeds exotic seeds as they are easily kept well during the space breeding journey.

2. According to the article, why is it important that we research and make discoveries in space seed breeding?

   A. A lot of money can be made by selling food to other countries.

B. Space seed breeding can contribute to China's food security and environmental protection.

C. China has plans to colonize mars in the near future.

D. In order to diversify the taste of food.

3 Which word below is not a synonym of "enhance"?

A. Heighten.

B. Enlarge.

C. Boost.

D. Contribute.

Do your research and answer these questions orally or by writing.

1 What are the differences between traditional and space seed breeding?

2 How can space seed breeding yield nearly 1,000 new species? What factors contributed to this result?

3 What do you think the author means by "seeds are as important as chips in the semiconductor industry"?

Shanghai adopts China's 1st provincial-level AI law to support sound, safe development

(2022.9.22)

Shanghai's **municipal legislature** on Thursday passed the country's first provincial-level law covering the development of **artificial intelligence** (AI), which experts said would effectively fill a gap where there was no specific law for AI and further pave the way for sound and **sustainable** development of technology.

At a meeting, the Shanghai Municipal People's Congress Standing Committee passed the Shanghai Regulations on Promoting the Development of the AI Industry, after public opinion was **solicited** from August 30 to September 13. The ordinance will come into effect on October 1.

One highlight of the new law is that it **stipulates** that the **relevant** municipal departments can draw up lists of "minor **illegalities**" in the development of the AI sector, indicating that there would be no **administrative** punishment for minor violations **in accordance with** the law as part of the government's efforts to encourage exploration and **stimulate** innovation.

一、背景简介

上海市十五届人大常委会第四十四次会议表决通过了《上海市促进人工智能产业发展条例》。条例于10月1日起实施，这是人工智能领域的首部省级地方性法规。此次立法立足于促进法的基本定位，注重创新性和引领性，充分发挥有效市场和有为政府的作用，采取各种激励措施推动人工智能产业高质量发展。这也是上海继《上海市数据条例》后的第二部数字经济领域地方法规，将有力支撑城市全面数字化转型，助力建成具有国际影响力的人工智能"上海高地"。

二、全文翻译

上海通过中国人工智能领域的首部省级地方性法规,支持人工智能行业健康安全发展

上海市人大常委会周四通过了全国首部涉及人工智能发展领域的省级地方性法规,专家表示,该法规将有效填补人工智能具体法律空白,进一步为技术的健康和可持续发展奠定基础。

在 8 月 30 日至 9 月 13 日征求公众意见后,上海市人大常委会在会议上通过了《上海市促进人工智能产业发展条例》。该条例将于 10 月 1 日起施行。

新法规的一个亮点是,它规定了市有关部门可以就人工智能产业发展过程中的轻微违法行为制定清单,这表明了政府为鼓励探索和刺激创新作出努力,将不会对轻微违法行为进行行政处罚。

三、单词点津

1. **municipal** [mjuːˈnɪsɪpl] *adj.* 市政的;地方自治的
2. **legislature** [ˈledʒɪsleɪtʃə(r)] *n.* 立法机关;立法机构
3. **artificial intelligence** 人工智能
4. **solicit** [səˈlɪsɪt] *v.* 请求,索求,征求
5. **stipulate** [ˈstɪpjuleɪt] *v.* 规定,明确要求
6. **relevant** [ˈreləvənt] *adj.* 有关的,切题的;有价值的
7. **illegality** [ˌɪliˈɡæləti] *n.* 违法;[法]非法行为
8. **administrative** [ədˈmɪnɪstrətɪv] *adj.* 管理的,行政的
9. **in accordance with** 依照;与……一致
10. **stimulate** [ˈstɪmjuleɪt] *v.* 促进,激发

四、练习题

1. According to the article, which of the following statements is true?

   A. The new law about AI has filled the gap and established a better way for responsible and maintainable development of technology.

B. The Shanghai Regulations on Promoting the Development of the AI Industry is to depress the development of the artificial intelligence industry in China.

C. The Shanghai Regulations on Promoting the Development of the AI Industry have been passed directly without any public opinion solicited.

D. According to the new law, any violation will be punished in accordance with the law as part of the government's efforts to innovation.

2. According to the article, which is the reason as to why there will be no administrative punishment for minor violations?

A. The new law enhances sustainable development of AI technology.

B. If you receive a punishment for every small violation, no one will join this industry.

C. The regulations are aimed at making the development of AI more sound.

D. The government is dedicated to promoting exploration and innovation.

3. Which word below is not a synonym of "solicit"?

A. Develop.

B. Appeal.

C. Seek.

D. Request.

Do your research and answer these questions orally or by writing.

1. How important do you think new laws are to new industries and why?

2. Why do you think the new law regulates that there will be no administrative punishment for minor violations?

China to cut soybean meal in livestock feed to ensure food security

(2022.9.20)

Major Chinese hog farmers and **feedstock** producers on Tuesday explained their efforts to cut down soybean meal use in a bid to lower the country's dependence on the crop and ensure the nation's food security.

Muyuan Foods Co, a leading hog and pork producer, said the company saved 1.3 million tons of soybean meal compared with the **average** level by using just 6.9 percent of soybean meal in its **compound** feed for pig breeding in 2021.

New Hope Liuhe, China's major feedstock producer, said it used just 10.7 percent soybean meal in its feed products in 2021, about 4.6 percentage points lower than the industry average, **equivalent** to reducing soybean meal **consumption** by 1.3 million tons.

The examples were cited after the Ministry of Agriculture and Rural Affairs (MOA) on Monday which vowed to **comprehensively** reduce the use of soybean meal in feed amid efforts to ensure national food security.

The MOA pointed out that the reduction is aimed at ensuring China's food security amid uncertain **external** supplies and promoting high-quality development and efficiency of the industry.

一、背景简介

中国正在努力加强粮食安全，举措之一是设法减少用于动物饲料的豆粕数量。中国农业农村部指出，粮食安全的最突出矛盾在饲料粮。它强调把豆粕等饲料粮减量替代的潜力充分发挥出来，保障饲料粮供给，维护粮食安全。中国目前是世界上最大的大豆进口国，2021 年大豆进口额超过 500 亿美元。随着世界面临通胀压力，食品进口成本进一步上升。因此，大豆消费量的改变也会有助于控制进口成本和通胀。2021 年，全国养殖业消耗的饲料中豆粕占比降到 15.3%，比 2017 年下降 2.5 个百分点，节约豆粕 1,100 万吨，折合大豆 1,400 万吨。

二、全文翻译

中国将减少牲畜饲料中的豆粕，以确保粮食安全

周二，中国主要生猪养殖企业和饲料生产商解释了他们如何尽量减少豆粕使用，以降低国家对大豆的依赖，确保国家粮食安全。

生猪养殖和猪肉生产巨头牧原食品股份有限公司表示，2021 年，公司在养猪复合饲料中仅使用了 6.9% 的豆粕，与平均水平相比，节省了 130 万吨豆粕。

中国主要饲料生产商新希望六和表示，2021 年其饲料产品中仅使用了 10.7% 的豆粕，比行业平均水平低约 4.6 个百分点，相当于减少了 130 万吨豆粕使用量。

周一，中国农业农村部（MOA）承诺在确保国家粮食安全的同时，全面减少豆粕在饲料中的使用，并引用了以上企业的例子。

农业农村部指出，此举措旨在让中国在外部供应不确定的情况下确保粮食安全，并促进该行业的高质量发展，提高效率。

三、单词点津

1. **feedstock** ['fi:dstɒk] *n.* 原料；给料
2. **average** ['ævərɪdʒ] *n.* 平均水平；平均值　*adj.* 普通的，平常的
3. **compound** ['kɒmpaʊnd] *n.* 混合物；化合物　*adj.* 复合的
4. **equivalent** [ɪ'kwɪvələnt] *adj.* 等同的；等效的　*n.* 对等的人（或事物）
5. **consumption** [kən'sʌmpʃn] *n.* 消费；消耗；食用

6 **comprehensively** [ˌkɒmprɪˈhensɪvli] *adv.* 包括一切地，完全地；全面地

7 **external** [ɪkˈstɜːnl] *adj.* 外部的，外面的；对外的

四、难句解析

New Hope Liuhe, China's major feedstock producer, said it used just 10.7 percent soybean meal in its feed products in 2021, about 4.6 percentage points lower than the industry average, equivalent to reducing soybean meal consumption by 1.3 million tons.

1 **China's major feedstock producer** 作插入语，是对前面名词的解释。

2 **4.6 percentage points lower than**，意为"比……低了4.6个百分点"。

3 **be equivalent to**，意为"等于，相当于"。

五、练习题

1 According to the article, which of the following statements is correct?

   A. In order to reduce national food security, the Ministry of Agriculture and Rural Affairs have to reduce the use of soybean meal.

   B. In an effort to rely more on this cheap crop, major Chinese hog farmers and feedstock producers put in efforts to add soybean meal.

   C. The reduction in soybean used in hog feed is important in order to increase food security.

   D. New Hope Liuhe used 10.7 percent soybean in 2021,

about 4.6 percentage points more than the industry average.

2. Which sentence is the wrong usage of "consumption"?

   A. The consumption of soybeans is a very important topic in regard to food security.

   B. Most of the wine was unfit for human consumption.

   C. We need to order more books for the library due to the student's consumption.

   D. The average daily consumption of vegetables and fruit is around 300 grams.

3. Which word below is not a synonym of "compound"?

   A. Mixture.

   B. Combination.

   C. Blend.

   D. Compromise.

Do your research and answer these questions orally or by writing.

1. How important is national food security and why? What can we do to protect it?

2. Why do you think there is such a focus specifically on soybeans?

Autonomous driving startups enhance tech innovation as industry gears up growth

(2022.9.15)

Chinese self-driving **startups** are enhancing technology innovation as China becomes the world's top market for smarter cars.

An **autonomous** driving startup Haomo.AI said on Wednesday that it had delivered three new sets of products for passenger vehicles in the past two and a half years, and that a version equipped with urban NOH (Navigation on HPilot) would enter mass production in September.

The carrying rate of high-level assisted driving will **exceed** 70 percent by 2025, according to Zhang Kai, chairman of Haomo.AI.

Meanwhile, off the back of huge demand for large model training, the company launched a supercomputing center to cut training cost and released China's first large-scale automated driving **scenario** library based on intelligent vehicle cooperative systems, in a bid to further **accelerate** the growth of China's automated driving sector.

In terms of automatic distribution of **terminal** logistics, the company launched an updated version of its **propriety** system, which has already entered mass production.

一、背景简介

智能车辆是一个集环境感知、规划决策、多等级辅助驾驶等功能于一体的综合系统,它集中运用了计算机、现代传感、信息融合、通信、人工智能及自动控制等技术,是典型的高新技术综合体。对智能车辆的研究主要致力于提高汽车的安全性、舒适性,以及提供优良的人车交互界面。近年来，智能车辆已经成为世界车辆工程领域研究的热点和汽车工业增长的新动力，很多发达国家都将其纳入各自重点发展的智能交通系统当中。本文对智能汽车领域的初创公司毫末在自动驾驶技术中的创新进行了介绍。

二、全文翻译

随着行业加速发展，自动驾驶初创企业加强技术创新

随着中国成为全球智能汽车的最大市场，中国的自动驾驶初创公司正在加强技术创新。

周三，自动驾驶初创公司毫末智行表示，在过去两年半里，公司已经交付了三套新的乘用车产品，搭载了城市NOH（智慧领航辅助系统）的版本将于9月开始量产。

据毫末董事长张凯介绍，到2025年，高级别辅助驾驶搭载率将超过70%。

与此同时，大模型训练需求量巨大，在此背景下，该公司推出了一个超级计算中心，以降低训练成本，并发布了中国首个基于智能汽车协作系统的大型自动驾驶场景库，进一步加速中国自动驾驶行业的发展。

在末端物流自动配送方面，该公司推出了其专有系统的更新版本，该系统已经进入批量生产。

三、单词点津

1. **startups** ['stɑːtʌps] *n.* 初创公司
2. **autonomous** [ɔːˈtɒnəməs] *adj.* 有自治权的；自主的；自动的。
   autonomous region 自治区
3. **exceed** [ɪkˈsiːd] *v.* 超过；超越（限制）；优于
4. **scenario** [səˈnɑːriəʊ] *n.* 设想；可能发生的情况；（电影、戏剧等）剧情梗概；（艺术或文学作品中的）场景
5. **accelerate** [əkˈseləreɪt] *v.* （使）加快，促进
6. **terminal** [ˈtɜːmɪnl] *n.* （火车、公共汽车或船的）终点站；航站楼；终端
7. **propriety** [prəˈpraɪəti] *n.* （行为，道德）正当，得体

四、难句解析

In terms of automatic distribution of terminal logistics, the company launched an updated version of its propriety system, which has already entered mass production.

1. **in terms of**，意为"就……而言，在……方面"。
2. **which** 引导非限定性定语从句，修饰 an updated version of system。

五、练习题

1. According to the article, which of the following statements is true?

   A. With the enhanced tech innovation, China becomes the second largest market for smarter cars.

   B. The carrying rate of high-level assisted driving will exceed 70 percent by 2021 and 80 percent by 2022.

   C. China's first large-scale automated driving scenario library will enhance the growth of China's automated driving sector.

   D. With diminished demand for large model training, the company established a large computing center to cut training models.

2. Which sentence has the wrong usage of "exceed"?

   A. The cost exceeded our estimate.

   B. He is trying to exceed last year's score.

   C. The demand for housing exceeded the supply.

   D. We all hope that we will exceed in the game this Saturday.

3 Which word can not replace "accelerate" in the article?

A. Harry.

B. Increase.

C. Speed.

D. Hurry.

Do your research and answer these questions orally or by writing.

1 Do you think that autonomous cars will replace traditional cars? What would you think if we didn't need to own a car and autonomous cars were centralized, allocated and deployed?

2 If autonomous driving systems were complete, do you think it would still be important to learn how to drive? In the future, what other skills do you think people will need to learn and what skills can people forget?

NEVs penetration rate to reach 25% this year

(2022.9.6)

Miao Wei, the former head of the Ministry of Industry and Information Technology (MIIT), said on Tuesday that the target of a 25-percent **penetration rate** of the new energy vehicles (NEVs) in China's road **fleet** could be achieved at the end of 2022, three years ahead of schedule.

The New-Energy Vehicle Industry Development Plan (2021-2035) released by **the State Council**, the cabinet, in November 2020 said that sales of NEVs will reach about 20 percent of total new vehicle sales by 2025.

China has witnessed a **booming** NEV consumption with the past couple of years. The penetration rate was less than 1 percent 10 years ago.

Sales of NEVs in 2012 were only 20,000 units. But at the end of May this year, NEVs running on road reached 11.08 million. China's production and sales of NEVs have ranked first in the world every year since 2015, according to Xin Guobin, deputy head of the MIIT.

Among the world's top 10 **best-selling** NEVs last year, Chinese brands accounted for six. Among the top 10 companies in terms of power battery **shipments**, Chinese battery makers held six places, Xin noted.

一、背景简介

新能源汽车是指采用非常规的车用燃料作为动力来源（或使用常规的车用燃料、采用新型车载动力装置），综合车辆的动力控制和驱动方面的先进技术，形成的技术原理先进、具有新技术、新结构的汽车。2020年11月，国务院办公厅印发《新能源汽车产业发展规划(2021—2035

年)》,要求深入实施发展新能源汽车国家战略,推动中国新能源汽车产业高质量可持续发展,加快建设汽车强国。截至 2021 年 5 月底,据中国汽车工业协会公布的数据,我国新能源汽车保有量约 580 万辆,约占全球新能源汽车总量的 50%。

二、全文翻译

今年,新能源汽车渗透率将达到 25%

工业和信息化部(MIIT)原部长苗圩周二表示,新能源汽车(NEV)在中国汽车市场渗透率达到 25% 的目标可能在 2022 年年底实现,比计划提前三年。

国务院 2020 年 11 月发布的《新能源汽车产业发展规划(2021—2035 年)》中明确,到 2025 年,新能源汽车的销量将达到新生产汽车总销量的 20% 左右。

近几年来,中国的新能源汽车消费蓬勃发展。10 年前新能源汽车的渗透率还不到 1%。

2012 年新能源汽车的销量仅为 2 万辆。但今年 5 月底,新能源汽车的累计销量达到了 1,108 万辆。工信部副部长辛国斌表示,自 2015 年以来,中国新能源汽车的生产和销售每年都位居世界第一。

在去年全球十大最畅销新能源汽车车型中,有六款是中国品牌车型。辛国斌指出,在动力电池装机量前十的企业中,我国占六席。

三、单词点津

1. **penetration rate** 渗透率,是对市场上当前需求和潜在市场需求的一种比较。市场渗透是企业发展战略的一种,即立足于现有产品,充分开发其市场潜力的企业发展战略。

2. **fleet** [fli:t] *n.* 船队;车队

3. **the State Council** 国务院

4. **booming** ['bu:mɪŋ] *adj.* 飞速发展的,繁荣的

5. **best-selling** [best 'selɪŋ] *adj.* 畅销的,抢手的

6. **shipment** ['ʃɪpmənt] *n.* 发货;运载的货物

四、练习题

1　According to the article, which of the following statements is true?

　　A. China has 10 best-selling NEVs brands and 10 power battery shipment companies.

　　B. China's production and sales of NEVs ranked first in the world, selling 11.08 million at the end of May this year.

　　C. With the penetration rate less than 1 percent 10 years ago, China has seen a downgrade in NEV consumption within the past decade.

　　D. China's road fleet could be achieved three years ahead of schedule.

2　What percentage of new vehicle sales does the New-Energy Vehicle Industry Development Plan aim to achieve by 2025?

　　A. 20,000 units.

　　B. Somewhere around twenty percent.

　　C. A quarter of the new vehicles sold.

　　D. One-third of the new vehicles sold.

3　Which word below is not a synonym of "booming"?

　　A. Roaring.

　　B. Thriving.

　　C. Prosperous.

　　D. Blocking.

Do your research and answer these questions orally or by writing.

1　What is considered sustainable energy? What other industries could benefit from sustainable energy?

2　What are the advantages of having more electric vehicles running on the roads?

China's power supply, energy structure tested in extreme drought amid transition to cleaner energy future

(2022.8.23)

As the rare **triple-dip La Nina** treks the globe leaving behind it extreme weather **phenomena** and disasters, some regions in southern China are experiencing a severe **drought** that only happens once in decades, which has challenged the country's power supply and **storage** system.

Southwest China's Sichuan Province, which largely relies on hydropower, has been facing the severest difficulties in history in ensuring power supply in recent weeks due **a triad of** challenges of extreme high temperatures, record low **precipitation**, and high power demands in the same period.

Moreover, by mid-August, about 12.32 million mu (821,333 hectares) of arable land had been hit by the drought along the Yangtze River, prompting the Ministry of Water Resources' urgent deployment of resources to ensure **irrigation**.

China has a robust system of power generation, transmission, and storage, as well as well-developed water irrigation infrastructures through constructing different water **conservancy** projects according to the resources and **geographical** conditions of diverse regions. It is also leading the world in developing new energies.

一、背景简介

四川是中国最大的水电开发和"西电东送"基地,肩挑着全国能源电力供应安全的重担。但在极端高温干旱天气的持续干扰下,"天府之国"

来水骤降，水力发电遭"腰斩"，急需省外电力的支援。2022年8月21日，四川启动突发事件能源供应保障一级应急响应，这是当地能源供应保障预警划分级别中的最高级。

和中国一样，2022年入夏以来，欧洲出现持续性高温天气，大部分地区较以往更加干燥，一些国家的降水量跌破纪录。高温干旱在导致用电需求大增的同时，对电力生产造成严重影响，令欧洲电力短缺困局继续恶化。如何提高电力系统抗灾能力是一道世界级难题。

二、全文翻译

在向清洁能源过渡期间，中国的电力供应、能源结构经受了极端干旱的考验

随着罕见的"三重"拉尼娜现象在全球范围内肆虐，极端的天气现象和灾害频发，中国南方的一些地区正在经历几十年一遇的严重干旱，这给中国的电力供应和储存系统带来了挑战。

中国西南部的四川省主要依靠水力发电，近几周来，由于极端高温、降水量骤降以及同期高电力需求的三重挑战，该省在确保电力供应方面遭遇历史上最大的困难。

此外，截至8月中旬，长江沿岸约有1,232万亩（821,333公顷）的耕地受到旱灾的影响，水利部紧急部署资源以确保灌溉。

中国拥有强大的发电、输电和储存系统，并根据不同地区的资源和地理条件，通过建设不同的水利工程，发展完善的水利基础设施。中国在开发新能源方面也处于世界领先地位。

三、单词点津

1. **triple-dip** 三次

2. **La Nina** 拉尼娜现象，指赤道太平洋东部和中部海表温度大范围持续异常变冷的现象，也称为反厄尔尼诺现象。

3. **phenomena** [fɪˈnɒmɪnə] *n.* 现象（phenomenon 的复数形式）

4. **drought** [draʊt] *n.* 旱灾，长期缺乏，严重短缺

5. **storage** ['stɔ:rɪdʒ] *n.* 储存，贮藏；（信息的）存储，存储空间
6. **a triad of** 三种
7. **precipitation** [prɪˌsɪpɪ'teɪʃn] *n.* 降水；降水量
8. **irrigation** [ˌɪrɪ'geɪʃən] *n.* 灌溉
9. **conservancy** [kən'sɜ:vənsi] *n.* 管理；保护，保存
10. **geographical** [ˌdʒi:ə'græfɪkl] *adj.* 地理的；地理学的

四、难句解析

Moreover, by mid-August, about 12.32 million mu (821,333 hectares) of arable land had been hit by the drought along the Yangtze River, prompting the Ministry of Water Resources' urgent deployment of resources to ensure irrigation.

1. **by** 加过去的时间点，主句要用过去完成时；by + 现在的时间点，主句用现在完成时；by 加将来的时间点，主句用将来完成时。本句是第一种情况。

2. **prompting** 动词的现在分词作状语，用来进一步说明谓语动词或整个句子的动作或状态，可以表示时间、原因、结果、目的、条件、方式、状况等。这里是对干旱情况导致结果的进一步说明。

五、练习题

1. According to the article, which of the following statements is correct?

   A. The Sichuan province largely relies on power by water.

   B. The infrastructure and system to deal with the extreme weather is not complete.

   C. Sichuan Province has been facing multiple disasters including bush fire, high temperatures, hydropower, and high power demands.

D. With the triple-dip La Nina treks, China is experiencing a severe drought that happens often.

2 According to the article, which has Southwest China's Sichuan Province not experienced?

A. Severe difficulties.

B. High temperature.

C. Low precipitation.

D. Tornado.

3 Which word below is not a synonym of "storage"?

A. Cache.

B. Stockpile.

C. Depot.

D. Deposition.

Do your research and answer these questions orally or by writing.

1 What are natural disasters and what do you know about them?

2 Have you experienced or heard of extreme weather? How do people deal with it?

第五部分 外交

扫一扫，听音频

Diplomacy

第1篇

Responsible neighbor: China maintains water release to downstream Mekong countries despite extreme heat, drought

(2022.8.29)

Despite extreme heat, drought, and water **shortages** that saw an obvious reduction in rainfall in Lancang River, China has **nevertheless** maintained water supply to the **lower reaches** of the Mekong River, the *Global Times* recently learned from the operator of key **hydropower** stations on China's Lancang River, on the **upper reaches** of the Mekong River which connects six countries.

Experts warn that extreme weather and droughts will possibly be the biggest challenge to Lancang-Mekong water resources currently, while some foreign countries outside the region such as the US take the chance to sow seeds of **discord** or **hype up** conflicts among the six **riparian** countries along the Lancang-Mekong River.

The envoys and representatives of the Mekong countries have called for enhanced cooperation and information sharing to bring the Lancang-Mekong Cooperation (LMC) **mechanism** to an elevated level despite Western **provocation** of ties.

一、背景简介

中方宣布将从 2020 年开始，与湄公河国家分享澜沧江全年水文信息，共建澜湄水资源合作信息共享平台，更好应对气候变化和洪旱灾害。中国作为负责任的合作伙伴，及时透明地与下游国家共享澜沧江水文信息，促进洪旱灾害管理等方面的务实合作，这起到了增信释疑、凝聚共识的重要作用，有助于推动提升各国水资源管理能力，促进未来区域间水资源的可持续开发与利用，为河流两岸人民生活带来更多福祉。澜湄合作不仅给六国人民带来了实实在在的利益，更成为世界范围内次区域合作的一道亮丽风景。

二、全文翻译

负责任邻国：尽管遭遇旱情，中国仍继续向湄公河下游国家补水

中国澜沧江位于连接六国的湄公河上游，《环球时报》从澜沧江重要水电站获悉，尽管酷暑、干旱和水资源短缺导致澜沧江降雨量明显减少，中国仍对湄公河下游国家保持供水。

专家警告说，极端天气和干旱可能是目前澜沧江—湄公河水资源面临的最大挑战，而美国等一些域外国家则趁机在澜沧江—湄公河沿岸的六国之间散布矛盾和激发冲突。

湄公河国家的特使和代表呼吁，要无视西方挑衅，加强合作和信息共享，使澜沧江—湄公河合作（LMC）机制更上一个台阶。

三、单词点津

1. **shortage** [ˈʃɔːtɪdʒ] *n.* 短缺；不足
2. **nevertheless** [ˌnevəðəˈles] *adv.* 尽管如此，然而，不过
3. **lower reaches**（河流）下游；**upper reaches** 上游
4. **hydropower** [ˈhaɪdrəʊˌpaʊə] *n.* 水力发电
5. **discord** [ˈdɪskɔːd] *n.* 意见分歧，不和
6. **hype up** 刺激；煽动
7. **riparian** [raɪˈpeərɪən] *adj.* 河边的；水滨的

8 **mechanism** [ˈmekənɪzəm] *n.* 机械装置；途径，方法；机制

9 **provocation** [ˌprɒvəˈkeɪʃn] *n.* 激怒，挑衅

四、难句解析

难句

Despite extreme heat, drought, and water shortages that saw an obvious reduction in rainfall in Lancang River, China has nevertheless maintained water supply to the lower reaches of the Mekong River.

1 **despite** 用作介词时，与 in spite of 同义，都表示"尽管""虽然""不顾"之意，放在句首时，要接成分，比如词或词组等。

2 **nevertheless** 在本句中用作连词。也可用作副词，常见句式为"…; nevertheless, …"。

五、练习题

选择题

1 According to the article, which statement is incorrect?

　A. No matter what natural disaster, China has still maintained water supply to the lower reaches of the Mekong River.

　B. Experts said that terrible weather and droughts would be the biggest challenge to Lancang-Mekong water resources.

　C. With China on the upper reaches of the Mekong River, the river connects six countries.

　D. Enhanced cooperation and information sharing will bring the Lancang-Mekong Cooperation (LMC) mechanism to an elevated level against the destructive effect from the whole world.

2 Why is it important that China maintains water supply from the Mekong River to other countries connecting with the Mekong River?

　A. Because of the Enhanced cooperation and information

sharing.

B. Because of the extreme heat, drought, and water shortages.

C. Because China is on the upper reaches of the Mekong River.

D. Because of the obvious reduction in rainfall in Lancang River.

3 Which is not a synonym of "discord"?

A. Conflict.

B. Harmony.

C. Disagreement.

D. Dispute.

Do your research and answer these questions orally or by writing.

1 What can we do as humans to deal with extreme weather?

2 Why is it important for people to protect rivers?

China to play important role in further development of SCO: former Uzbek deputy prime minister

(2022.9.21)

The role of China as one of the founding members of the **Shanghai Cooperation Organization (SCO)** is enormous in its **formation** and further development and it continues to be the leading factor in **facilitating** economic and trade cooperation within the SCO, former Uzbek deputy prime minister and former minister of foreign affairs of Uzbekistan Saidkasimov Saidmukhtar told the *Global Times* in an **exclusive** interview.

Uzbekistan chaired the SCO summit this year in Samarkand. The event, which took place from September 15–16, attracted worldwide attention, as it was one of the most **prominent** events held in Central Asia with the participation of many world leaders. The summit was a great success for the new open and **constructive** foreign policy of the President of Uzbekistan Sh.Mirziyoyev.

"The significance of the Samarkand summit was also determined by the fact that the total territory of the SCO countries occupies about 40 percent of the world, in which one third of humanity now lives. Their share is more than a quarter of world GDP, while their economic growth rates are much higher than global **indicators**," said Saidkasimov.

一、背景简介

2022 年对中亚各国和中国都是具有里程碑意义的一年。30 年前，中国是最早与独立后的中亚五个共和国建立外交关系的国家之一，也开启了中国与中亚五国友好关系史上的一个新时代。乌兹别克斯坦（简称：乌）与中国的友谊历史可以追溯到伟大的"丝绸之路"。由于两国领导人之间的高度互信,在睦邻友好、相互理解和开放的原则基础上,两国积极发展经贸、投资、金融和技术、工业、人文等领域合作。中乌伙伴关系成为守望相助、睦邻友好的典范。

2022年9月15日至16日,上海合作组织成员国元首理事会第二十二次会议在乌兹别克斯坦历史名城撒马尔罕举行。中国国家主席习近平在大会上发表题为《把握时代潮流、加强团结合作、共创美好未来》的讲话,提出"上海合作组织作为国际和地区事务中重要建设性力量,要勇于面对国际风云变幻,牢牢把握时代潮流,不断加强团结合作,推动构建更加紧密的上海合作组织命运共同体"。

二、全文翻译

乌兹别克斯坦前副总理:中国将在上合组织进一步发展中发挥重要作用

乌兹别克斯坦前副总理兼前外交部部长赛义德卡西莫夫·赛义德穆赫塔尔在接受《环球时报》专访时表示,中国作为上海合作组织(上合组织)创始成员国之一,在其成立和进一步发展中发挥着巨大的作用,是促进上合组织内经贸合作的关键因素。

今年,乌兹别克斯坦在撒马尔罕主持了上合组织峰会。峰会于9月15日至16日举行,吸引了世界的关注。这是中亚地区最重要的活动之一,众多世界领导人出席峰会。乌兹别克斯坦总统米尔济约耶夫提出新的开放和建设性外交政策,峰会取得巨大成功。

赛义德卡西莫夫说:"撒马尔罕峰会的意义还基于这样一个事实,即上合组织国家的总领土约占世界的40%,拥有世界三分之一的人口,GDP所占的份额超过世界的四分之一,而经济增速远高于全球平均水平。"

三、单词点津

1. **Shanghai Cooperation Organization (SCO)** 上海合作组织起源于1996年成立的上海五国会晤机制,是中华人民共和国、俄罗斯联邦、哈萨克斯坦共和国、吉尔吉斯共和国、塔吉克斯坦共和国的关于加强边境地区信任和裁军的谈判进程的组织。2001年1月,乌兹别克斯坦提出作为正式成员加入上海五国。

2. **formation** [fɔːˈmeɪʃn] *n.* 组成物；构成；形成，产生

3. **facilitate** [fəˈsɪlɪteɪt] *v.* 使更容易，使便利；促进，推动

4. **exclusive** [ɪkˈskluːsɪv] *adj.* 独有的，专用的；昂贵的；排外的；独家的　*n.* 独家新闻

5. **prominent** [ˈprɒmɪnənt] *adj.* 重要的；著名的；显眼的

6. **constructive** [kənˈstrʌktɪv] *adj.* 建设性的；有助益的

7. **indicator** [ˈɪndɪkeɪtə(r)] *n.* 标志；迹象；方向灯

四、难句解析

The event, which took place from September 15–16, attracted worldwide attention, as it was one of the most prominent events held in Central Asia with the participation of many world leaders.

1. **which** 引导非限定性定语从句，修饰先行词"event"。
2. **as** 作连词，引导原因状语从句，表示"因为……"。

五、练习题

1. According to the article, which statement is correct?

   A. The SCO summit this year in Samarkand was one of the most important events held in Central Asia, with the participation of many world leaders.

   B. As the sole founding member of the Shanghai Cooperation Organization (SCO), China has enormous power in further development.

   C. China is an unimportant support factor in facilitating economic trade cooperation within the SCO.

   D. The importance of the Samarkand summit was determined

by the fact that the total territory of the SCO countries occupy about three fourths of the world.

2 About how much GDP do the countries involved in the SCO generate?

  A. More than 25% of world GDP.

  B. Half of the world GDP.

  C. Three quarters of the global income.

  D. The sum of China and Uzbekistan.

3 Which is not a synonym of "constructive"?

  A. Helpful.

  B. Useful.

  C. Worthwhile.

  D. Destructive.

Do your research and answer these questions orally or by writing.

1 What other world organization do you know about and what do they do?

2 What do you think about these types of global organizations and how do they influence people?

China and Pakistan 'true brothers sharing weal and woe'

(2022.9.20)

China and Pakistan have witnessed strengthened **bilateral** relations and more **extensive** cooperation in a range of fields, especially in the construction of the **China-Pakistan Economic Corridor (CPEC)**, which analysts pointed out helped lay the foundation for Pakistan's **sustained** economic modernization.

Meanwhile, the two countries have also demonstrated the spirit of support and true friendship amid **hardships**. "The Dasu Hydropower Project of China Gezhouba Group Company Limited organized a flood relief activity where the management made **donations** of almost 400 packages of food supplies to the local flood victims in order to help them **mitigate** their sufferings due to heavy floods," Chinese Ambassador to Pakistan Nong Rong wrote on Twitter on September 15.

This is one of the latest **consignment** of **humanitarian** relief goods that China sent to Pakistan as the country continues to suffer from the devastating impacts of floods in the nation which have led to more than 1,500 deaths and affected 33 million people.

一、背景简介

中国和巴基斯坦是全天候战略合作伙伴和"铁杆"朋友。建交 70 多年来，无论国际风云如何变幻，两国始终相互理解、相互信任、相互支持。近年来，两国在世界之变、时代之变、历史之变中并肩前行，携手应对新冠疫情和重大自然灾害挑战，高质量共建中巴经济走廊，深化全方位交流合作，就国际地区事务开展密切协调配合。巴基斯坦洪灾发生后，中国第一时间做出响应，向巴方提供急需帮助，支持巴方开展救灾工作。

二、全文翻译

中巴是"患难与共的真兄弟"

中国和巴基斯坦在一系列领域加强了双边关系和更广泛合作,特别是在中巴经济走廊(CPEC)建设方面,分析人士指出,这为巴基斯坦持续的经济现代化奠定了基础。

与此同时,两国也展现了患难见真情的精神。9月15日,中国驻巴基斯坦大使农融在推特上写道:"中国葛洲坝集团有限公司达苏水电站项目组织了洪灾救援活动,向当地洪灾灾民捐赠了近400包食品,帮助他们减轻洪灾带来的痛苦。"。

这是中国向巴基斯坦运送的最新一批人道主义救援物资之一。巴基斯坦还在遭受洪灾的破坏性影响,洪灾已导致1,500多人死亡,3,300万人受灾。

三、单词点津

1. **bilateral** [ˌbaɪˈlætərəl] *adj.* 双方的;双边的;(身体部位)两侧的
2. **extensive** [ɪkˈstensɪv] *adj.* 广阔的;广泛的;巨大的;大量的
3. **China-Pakistan Economic Corridor (CPEC)** 中巴经济走廊是前总理李克强于2013年5月访问巴基斯坦时提出的。初衷是加强中巴之间交通、能源、海洋等领域的交流与合作,加强两国互联互通,促进两国共同发展。该项目于2015年4月20日启动。
4. **sustained** [səsˈteɪnd] *adj.* 持续的,持久的;坚持不懈的
5. **hardship** [ˈhɑːdʃɪp] *n.* 困苦,艰难
6. **donation** [dəʊˈneɪʃn] *n.* 捐赠物;捐赠,赠送
7. **mitigate** [ˈmɪtɪɡeɪt] *v.* 减轻,缓和
8. **consignment** [kənˈsaɪnmənt] *n.* 发送的货物,运送物;发送,投递
9. **humanitarian** [hjuːˌmænɪˈteəriən] *adj.* 人道主义的;博爱的 *n.* 人道主义者

1. According to the article, which statement is correct?

   A. The China Gezhouba Group Company Limited made donations to the local flood victims in order to help them worsen their sufferings due to heavy floods.

   B. China and Pakistan have experienced enhanced bilateral relations and more extensive cooperation in many fields.

   C. China only donated packages of food to Pakistan as the country continues to suffer from the devastating impacts of floods.

   D. After China sent Pakistan the last consignment of humanitarian aid, Pakistan stopped suffering from the impacts of floods.

2. What is the reason behind China sending humanitarian aid to Pakistan?

   A. In order to increase the relationship between China and the Middle East.

   B. To help mitigate the negative impacts of the recent floods.

   C. Because China will receive something in return from Pakistan.

   D. The Pakistan people within China want to help.

3. Which is not a synonym of "mitigate"?

   A. Relieve.

   B. Deteriorate.

   C. Lessen.

   D. Alleviate.

Do your research and answer these questions orally or by writing.

1. Explain the China-Pakistan Economic Corridor (CPEC), what are some of its goals?

2. How do you understand true friendship between countries?

Commemorative activities held to voice hope for a constructive China-Japan relation

(2022.9.26)

As September 29 marks the 50th anniversary of the **normalization** of China-Japan diplomatic relations, people from various walks of life in China have held **commemorative** activities to review the progress and achievements of China-Japan exchanges over the last decades and look forward to constructive and stable bilateral relations.

A **symposium** on 50 years of China-Japan economic exchanges organized by the National Japanese Economic Association and Chinese Academy of Social Sciences was held in Beijing, bringing together more than 100 scholars and representatives from both China and Japan to provide valuable ideas and plans for the development of China-Japanese economic and trade relations through discussion.

In general, both China and Japan attach great importance to economic cooperation despite some problems and challenges. After 50 years of economic exchanges and cooperation, China and Japan have become **inseparable** partners with closely **integrated** industrial and supply chains. The two sides should work together to further deepen economic ties, Chen Yonghua, former Chinese ambassador to Japan, also executive vice president of the China-Japan Friendship Association, stated at the symposium.

一、背景简介

2022年是中日邦交正常化 50 周年，中日双方在政经等各个层面举行了多项纪念活动，表达了对推动中日关系沿着正确轨道健康稳定发展、构筑契合新时代要求的中日关系的期待。

第五部分 外交

　　2022年9月25日，由全国日本经济学会主办、中国社会科学院日本研究所承办的"全国日本经济学会2022年会暨中日经济交流50年研讨会"在京召开。在外部环境更趋严峻复杂和不确定的背景下，中日经贸合作面临诸多风险和挑战。50年来中日经贸合作取得巨大成就，《区域全面经济伙伴关系协定》（RCEP）的生效、世界经济复苏等对中日经贸合作的利好因素也在上升。100多位学者及媒体代表以线上线下结合方式出席了本次研讨会，意在对中日经济交流的过去、现在和未来进行系统的回顾和前瞻，对其中具有理论意义和实践价值的课题进行深入探讨，为中日经贸关系的发展提供有价值的思路与方案。

二、全文翻译

各界举办纪念活动，对建设性中日关系表示期盼

　　2022年9月29日是中日邦交正常化50周年纪念日，中国各界人士纷纷举行纪念活动，回顾过去几十年中日交往的进展和成就，期待两国关系健康稳定发展。

　　由全国日本经济学会和中国社会科学院组织的中日经济交流50年研讨会在北京举行，来自中日两国的100多名学者和代表齐聚一堂，展开热烈讨论，为中日经贸关系发展提供了宝贵的思路和方案。

　　总的来说，尽管存在一些问题和挑战，但中日两国都非常重视经济合作。经过50年的经济交流与合作，中日两国已成为密不可分的合作伙伴，产业链和供应链紧密结合。中日友好协会常务副会长、中国原驻日大使程永华在研讨会上表示，双方应共同努力，进一步深化经济联系。

三、单词点津

1. **normalization** [ˌnɔːməlaɪˈzeɪʃən] *n.* 正常化；标准化
2. **commemorative** [kəˈmemərətɪv] *adj.* 纪念的
3. **symposium** [sɪmˈpəʊziəm] *n.* 专题研讨会，讨论会
4. **inseparable** [ɪnˈsepərəbl] *adj.* （人）形影不离的；（东西）分不开的，不可分离的
5. **integrated** [ˈɪntɪɡreɪtɪd] *adj.* 各部分密切协调的；综合的，整合的

四、难句解析

In general, both China and Japan attach great importance to economic cooperation despite some problems and challenges.

① 常用短语"**both…and…**"意为"……与……两个都",注意动词用复数形式。

② **attach great importance to**,意为"非常重视"。

③ **despite** 介词"尽管",后面接名词或词组。

五、练习题

① According to the article, which statement is true?

   A. The 50th anniversary of the normalization of China-Japan diplomatic relations reviewed the advancements and achievements of exchanges over the last century.

   B. A symposium on 50 years of China-Japan economic exchanges was held in Beijing, bringing together more than 100 scholars and representatives from China to provide valuable ideas and plans.

   C. After 50 years of economic exchanges and cooperation, China and Japan have become divisible partners with segregated industrial and supply chains.

   D. Even with many obstacles, close cooperation is important for both China and Japan.

② Which is the correct explanation of "people from various walks of life"?

   A. People from different places.

   B. People who talk different dialects.

C. People who have different careers.

D. All of the above.

3. Which of the following activity is not a commemorative activity?

A. Opening Ceremony.

B. Anniversary.

C. Birthday party.

D. Concert.

Do your research and answer these questions orally or by writing.

1. What do you know about the history between Japan and China? What do you think the future holds for the future relationship between the two countries?

2. What are some of the similarities and differences between China and Japan?

LMC mechanism provides blueprint for successful bilateral relations as China, Myanmar treasure friendship: Myanmar politician

(2022.8.30)

The China-initiated Lancang-Mekong Cooperation (LMC) is one of the most effective **avenues** of cooperation between China and Myanmar, the secretary-general of the Democratic Party of Myanmar, Than Than Nu, told the *Global Times* recently in an interview. As a diplomat and daughter of Myanmar's first prime minister U Nu, she has made at least five visits to China, and was impressed by China's great achievements, and the Communist Party of China (CPC)'s **unremitting** efforts toward safeguarding people's wellbeing.

Than Than Nu believes that China's success may act as a useful reference for Myanmar in economic development, the improvement of people's livelihoods, and **poverty eradication**.

"On my father's first meeting with Chairman Mao Zedong, he told my father that the Chinese government had launched one hundred development projects and hoped that with their completion, China would be able to assist Myanmar to a **considerable** extent. Now the avenues of cooperation between the two countries have increased annually and one of them, the LMC, I should say, is the most effective one," Than Than Nu told the *Global Times*.

一、背景简介

2014年11月，国务院前总理李克强在第十七次中国—东盟领导人会议上提出建立澜沧江—湄公河合作（简称"澜湄合作"）机制。2016年3月，澜湄合作首次领导人会议在海南三亚举行，全面启动澜湄合作进程。2018年1月，澜湄合作第二次领导人会议在柬埔寨金边举行，标志澜湄合作从培育期迈向成长期。

澜湄合作机制旨在深化六国睦邻友好关系和务实合作，促进沿岸各国经济社会发展，打造澜湄流域经济发展带，共建澜湄国家命运共同体；增进各国人民福祉，助力东盟共同体建设和地区一体化进程，为推进南南合作和落实联合国2030年可持续发展议程作出贡献。

二、全文翻译

缅甸政治家：澜湄合作机制为中缅两国友好关系绘制了蓝图

缅甸民主党秘书长丹丹努近日在接受《环球时报》采访时表示，中国发起的澜沧江—湄公河合作机制（LMC）是中缅两国最有效的合作渠道之一。丹丹努作为一名外交官，同时也是缅甸首任总理吴努的女儿，她对中国进行了至少五次访问，对中国取得的巨大成就和中国共产党为增进人民福祉所做的不懈努力印象深刻。

丹丹努认为，中国的成功可以为缅甸发展经济、改善民生和消除贫困提供有益借鉴。

丹丹努对《环球时报》记者表示："在我父亲第一次与毛泽东主席会面时，他告诉我父亲，中国政府已经启动了100个发展项目，并希望随着这些项目的完成，中国能够在很大程度上帮助缅甸。现在，两国之间的合作渠道每年都在增加，而澜沧江—湄公河合作机制是其中最有效的一个。"

三、单词点津

1. **avenue** ['ævənju:] *n.* 大街；（通向大宅子的）林荫道；途径，渠道

2. **unremitting** [ˌʌnrɪ'mɪtɪŋ] *adj.* 不停的，不懈的，持续不断的

3. **poverty** ['pɒvəti] *n.* 贫穷，贫困

4. **eradication** [ɪˌrædɪ'keɪʃn] *n.* 根除，消灭

5. **considerable** [kən'sɪdərəbl] *adj.* 相当大的；相当重要的

四、难句解析

On my father's first meeting with Chairman Mao Zedong, he told my father that the Chinese government had launched one hundred development projects and hoped that with their completion, China would be able to assist Myanmar to a considerable extent.

1. **tell sb. that** 中的 that 引导宾语从句，后面接完整句子即可。
2. **hope that** 同样引导宾语从句。
3. **to some extent**，意为"在某种程度上，在一定程度上"。

五、练习题

1. According to the article, which statement is correct?

   A. The prime minister of Myanmar has visited China at least five times.

   B. The prime minister's son serves as the secretary general of the Myanmar democratic party.

   C. Myanmar's diplomat is the prime minister's daughter and she has visited China five times.

   D. Myanmar is following China's footsteps in terms of the educational system.

2. What did Chairman Mao Zedong tell Than Than Nu's father?

   A. The Lancang-Mekong Cooperation (LMC) is one of the most effective avenues of cooperation between China and Myanmar.

   B. With the one hundred development projects' completion, China would be able to help Myanmar significantly.

C. Than Than Nu will be the secretary-general of the Democratic Party of Myanmar.

   D. Chairman Mao Zedong and Than Than Nu's father will meet every ten years' time.

3 Which is not a synonym of "eradication"?

   A. Erasure.

   B. Establishment.

   C. Removal.

   D. Elimination.

Do your research and answer these questions orally or by writing.

1 How important do you think the international relationship to a country is and why?

2 What should we do to improve international relationships in general?

Chinese UN representative reiterates opposition to bio weapons

(2022.10.28)

China firmly opposes research, development, **stockpiling** or the use of biological weapons by any country under any **circumstance**, Ambassador Geng Shuang, Deputy Permanent Representative of the People's Republic of China to the United Nations, **reiterated** at a briefing of the United Nations Security Council on Thursday over the biosecurity issue in Ukraine.

At the briefing, UN's High Representative for **Disarmament** Affairs Adedeji Ebo told the Council that Russia had filed a formal **complaint** over **allegations** of a biological weapons program in Ukraine under Article VI of the Biological Weapons Convention. And UN's High Representative for Disarmament Affairs, Izumi Nakamitsu, had previously informed ambassadors that the UN had seen no evidence of biological weapons use in Ukraine.

Reiterating that China firmly opposes research, development, stockpiling or the use of biological weapons by any country under any circumstances, Geng called on States parties to strictly **observe** the objectives and principles of the BWC.

一、背景简介

2022年10月27日，联合国安理会召开会议审议乌克兰生物安全问题。中方在会议发言中表示，中方坚决反对任何国家在任何情况下研发、储存或使用生物武器，同时呼吁国际社会尽早重启停滞20多年的《禁止生物武器公约》核查议定书谈判，切实提升全球生物安全水平。生物军事活动事关国际和平与安全，事关全人类共同利益。中方在二战期间深受生物武器之害，一贯主张全面禁止和彻底销毁包括生物武器在内的一切大规模杀伤性武器,坚决反对任何国家在任何情况下研发、储存或使用生物武器。所有缔约国都应严格遵守《禁止生物武器公约》的目标和原则。

二、全文翻译

中国常驻联合国代表重申:反对生物武器

周四,中国常驻联合国副代表、特命全权大使耿爽在联合国安理会关于乌克兰生物安全问题的简会上重申,中方坚决反对任何国家在任何情况下研发、储存或使用生物武器。

在简会上,联合国裁军事务高级代表阿德吉·埃博告诉安理会,俄罗斯已根据《禁止生物武器公约》第六条,就乌克兰生物武器计划的指控提出正式控诉。联合国裁军事务高级代表中满泉此前曾告知各国大使,联合国没有发现乌克兰使用生物武器的证据。

耿爽重申,中国坚决反对任何国家在任何情况下研发、储存或使用生物武器,呼吁缔约国严格遵守《禁止生物武器公约》的目标和原则。

三、单词点津

1. **stockpile** ['stɒkpaɪl] *n.* 库存,积蓄 *v.* 贮存,储蓄
2. **circumstance** ['sɜːkəmstəns] *n.* 条件;情况;环境
3. **reiterate** [riˈɪtəreɪt] *v.* 重申,反复说
4. **disarmament** [dɪsˈɑːməmənt] *n.* 裁减军备;解除武装
5. **complaint** [kəmˈpleɪnt] *n.* 抱怨,投诉
6. **allegation** [ˌæləˈgeɪʃn] *n.* 说法;指控
7. **observe** [əbˈzɜːv] *v.* 遵守;注意到,观察到;注视,监视

四、练习题

1. According to the article, which statement is correct?

A. China firmly stated that except extreme circumstance, any country should oppose research, stockpiling or the use of biological weapons.

B. UN's High Representative for Disarmament Affairs, Izumi Nakamitsu, had previously stated that the UN had seen little evidence of biological weapons use in Ukraine.

C. Ambassador Geng Shuang, Deputy Permanent Representative of the People's Republic of China gave a speech to the United Nations.

D. China decided on State parties to strictly observe the objectives and principles of the BWC.

2 Which of the following explanation is correct for "Disarmament"?

A. The removal and discontinuation of weapons.

B. To learn how to use weapons safely.

C. Only use these types of weapons when necessary.

D. Build a safe weapon's depot.

3 Which is not a synonym of "complaint"?

A. Grumble.

B. Accomplishment.

C. Whine.

D. Quibble.

问答题

Do your research and answer these questions orally or by writing.

1 What do you know about biological weapons and when were they used?

2 Why do you think China reiterated that we firmly oppose research, development, stockpiling, or the use of biological weapons by any country under any circumstances?

参考答案

第一部分　科技 Technology

第 1 篇：1. D　2. A　3. A　　　第 6 篇：1. C　2. A　3. B
第 2 篇：1. C　2. D　3. D　　　第 7 篇：1. C　2. A　3. A
第 3 篇：1. C　2. C　3. B　　　第 8 篇：1. C　2. A　3. B
第 4 篇：1. A　2. D　3. C　　　第 9 篇：1. B　2. B　3. D
第 5 篇：1. D　2. A　3. C

第二部分　社会 Society

第 1 篇：1. C　2. A　3. D　　　第 8 篇：1. D　2. B　3. C
第 2 篇：1. B　2. D　3. A　　　第 9 篇：1. B　2. C　3. D
第 3 篇：1. D　2. C　3. B　　　第 10 篇：1. D　2. C　3. D
第 4 篇：1. D　2. B　3. C　　　第 11 篇：1. D　2. D　3. D
第 5 篇：1. B　2. C　3. C　　　第 12 篇：1. A　2. D　3. D
第 6 篇：1. C　2. B　3. D　　　第 13 篇：1. D　2. C　3. A
第 7 篇：1. C　2. D　3. B

第三部分　文化 Culture

第 1 篇：1. D　2. B　3. D　　　第 7 篇：1. B　2. A　3. C
第 2 篇：1. B　2. A　3. C　　　第 8 篇：1. A　2. D　3. D
第 3 篇：1. D　2. A　3. C　　　第 9 篇：1. C　2. A　3. B
第 4 篇：1. D　2. A　3. C　　　第 10 篇：1. D　2. C　3. C
第 5 篇：1. B　2. A　3. C　　　第 11 篇：1. C　2. D　3. B
第 6 篇：1. D　2. C　3. C

第四部分　政经 Politics and Economy

第 1 篇：1. C　2. C　3. B　　第 6 篇：1. A　2. D　3. A
第 2 篇：1. C　2. D　3. A　　第 7 篇：1. C　2. C　3. D
第 3 篇：1. C　2. B　3. B　　第 8 篇：1. C　2. D　3. A
第 4 篇：1. D　2. C　3. C　　第 9 篇：1. B　2. B　3. B
第 5 篇：1. B　2. B　3. D　　第 10 篇：1. A　2. D　3. D

第五部分　外交 Diplomacy

第 1 篇：1. D　2. C　3. B　　第 4 篇：1. D　2. D　3. D
第 2 篇：1. A　2. A　3. D　　第 5 篇：1. C　2. B　3. B
第 3 篇：1. B　2. B　3. B　　第 6 篇：1. C　2. A　3. B